DUCKY

DUCKY

(A story of Donald and Phyllis)

Life Letters

MICHAEL W DYMOND

AuthorHouse™
1663 Liberty Drive
Bloomington, IN 47403
www.authorhouse.com
Phone: 1 (800) 839-8640

Published by AuthorHouse 3/11/2015

ISBN: 978-1-4969-7450-1 (sc)
ISBN: 978-1-4969-7449-5 (e)

Library of Congress Control Number: 2015903646

Print information available on the last page.

CONTENTS

FOREWORD

WAR: nothing new.

As a result of this war, many faced the same daunting challenge of families torn apart, lost love and simple survival. Each took up the call and accepted that challenge. Donald joined the war effort in order to protect a future which he felt strongly had been placed in jeopardy as a result of Hitler's bold attempt to make the world his.

Phyllis, a home body, desired that future, too, and with all her heart...wanting nothing else. Donald saw that this future may be threatened. His father, Robert, himself a veteran of WW1 with the RAF, may have been an encouragement for Donald to join Canada's active forces in July of 1940. Donald had for some time been involved with a local militia, The Kent Regiment, and felt compelled to do more.

Michael, Phyllis, Robert, Margo, Dorothy.

Phyllis and Donald started exchanging letters as early as 1938. They had been dating for about a year. Hundreds were written and exchanged, laden with laughter and love, promise and fear, and eternal hope through to Donald's untimely and heartbreaking death on April 30, 1945, just a mere ten days before VE Day in Europe.

These letters comprise the essence of this story through which I have struggled to make the conversation real, meaningful and enduring. My palpable challenge came when I realized very early that most of Phyllis' (Mom's letters) had been destroyed.

My intent, again, for this project was to create a story: a 'conversation' between two young people decidedly in love, recently married, with plans for a future together...but separated by preparations for war, and war itself. In one of his letters, Donald (Dad) said that his company's constant movement, while in training across Canada and the lack of safe storage, forced him eventually to burn the letters from Phyllis. Few survived. You, the reader, should know this.

As the writer and son, I knew my mother Phyllis first hand, but I only really got to know my father, Donald, over the years through many wonderful family stories and his wealth of astonishing letters. He poured every fiber of his love and devotion to his wife and family into each line and much of it day-to-day small talk which is the stuff of relationships. Every effort has been made to create a meaningful, informative and enjoyable read.

DEDICATION

To Donald and Phyllis: my Father and Mother.

Donald W Dymond, Circa 1935

Phyllis E Jackson, Circa 1932

ACKNOWLEDGEMENTS

Of singular importance are the letters as they became their life together. These truly were love letters that Dad and Mom, from 1938 through to the war's end, lovingly wrote to each other. In an attempt to capture their essence, style, structure, spelling and grammar remains as they wrote. Over four-hundred would be my guess, however, few of Mother's survived. It is from reading these that I saw and felt the undying love that bound them. It was a very deep and abiding adoration, that grew continually stronger in the waning days of the conflict when going home, and being home with those you love and miss, was all you could taste.

WARPATH The seminal work of Major G. L. Cassidy DSO, published in 1948. This landmark effort chronicled, in remarkable detail, the path of the Algonquin Regiment and its many members, NCOs and officers alike, from its creation in Ontario, Canada, through its tour of France, Belgium and Holland to the borders of Germany and the war's end.

Kristan Verhaeghe, my step-daughter, guided me through some Government of Canada online sites when I was researching my Dad's service record. She is exceptionally good at these processes and research in general. I thank her sincerely.

Wikipedia, for significant details about WWII and Canada's involvement, notwithstanding the political turmoil it underwent regarding its decision to declare war on Germany while still being a part of the British Commonwealth. The role played of supplying the many needs of the war effort during the conflict was momentous.

A special mention must go to Marianne King-Wilson of Parry Sound, Ontario, who, working with a very active local Algonquin Regiment, adopted my father in their splendid Adopt a Vet program for the 2014 Remembrance Day ceremony. During many delightful and informative email conversations with Marianne, it was her suggestion where I should start my story, as I was simply stuck. This provided the spark I needed to get underway and eventually complete this book.

During my research and with the brilliant assistance of Marianne King-Wilson (I am not great online) I discovered two distant cousins: Bob Carter of Australia and Austin Hind of England. Austin is currently serving with the Canadian forces in Manitoba, Canada. Their mere discovery overwhelmed me and added much impetus to my desire to write and complete this project.

No contribution is too small to recognize. My very good friend, Hugh Logan, of Chatham, Ontario and Chris Mann of Wallaceburg, Ontario both aided in the research of places from the 1940s in Chatham so crucial to the book's setting. I sincerely thank you both.

Last, but not least, are my editors: My wife, Mary, and our very close and dear friend Marcia Watters. Their professional business careers made them perfect fits for the editing and re-writing process. I cannot thank them enough for their patience and effort.

THE EARLY DAYS

Phyllis and Donald, Circa 1939

❦ Michael W Dymond ❦

September 17, 1938,
Oxford Group Camp,
Eastview, Kingston

Hello Darling:

How are you? I'll just write a few lines because I haven't much to say.

I just got back from Gananoque and the new bridge across the St Lawrence River, the one that President Roosevelt made the big speech at a little while ago, it's about 7 1/2 miles across – I didn't cross!

I'm looking forward to seeing you again, I sure am missing you.

It was quite cool here last night. We had exercises outside the first thing this morning & then we went for a swim, boy was it cold. I just got through shaving & almost mislaid a piece of my chin. tsk! tsk! tsk!

I hope you haven't been staying home too much and feeling blue, have a good time if you can & don't do anything I wouldn't do?? But I hope that is all through with now, & I'm going to try & make a new start when I get back.

Well Darling so-long for the time, I love you more since I've been away from you & I'll make up for it at the earliest possible moment. My heart is with you even if I can't hold you close to it.

Lots of love

Ducky!

ᘒ Ducky ᘒ

Dec. 14, 1938.
Eastview, Kingston, Ont.
Oxford Group Camp.

Dear Ducky P. U.

There happened to be a typewriter in my cottage and so I am taking advantage of it.

It is raining here and I am a little wet from coming up to the cottage from the hall, about a three minute walk. The hall where we hold our meetings is at the bottom of a hill and mine is no. 13. I have taken the job of seeing that the cottage is kept in good order and everything kept clean and neat.

You have no idea what a wonderful place this is, solely because of the marvelous bunch of fellows that are here. There are sixty-five or seventy here now and we are expecting probably two-hundred or more.

I mailed you a post card at noon but I thought I should write you a letter going into detail.

I am convinced there are a number of things that I must straighten out with you when I get back and I am looking forward to the time.

I hope everyone is getting along fine and that Shirley's situation has been coped with.

We got here safely on Monday. The three of us had headaches when we arrived due to fumes coming from the motor through a hole in the floor. Something went wrong with the starter today, it works but it doesn't connect with the motor – a little push will start it however.

Bob, another fellow, and myself were taken through a sort of a fortified structure near the Military College in Kingston

3

yesterday and it was really interesting to see the weapons that they used to use.

If you want to write to me you can address it to the above heading, and if you don't write I will understand.

The most amazing thing about this camp is the fact that we have here what the whole world wants, the answer to every problem of the world.

I don't seem to be going about the situation in the right way and I am therefore rather disappointed with myself. I am however beginning to get an idea of the outlay.

Well Darling, when I return I will tell you all about everything.

Until then I remain yours with the deepest love.

Don

ABOUT MOM AND DAD

Phyllis was born in Chatham, Ontario, Canada in 1916 and lived with her parents and younger sister, Shirley, at 23 Dover Street, a very modest part of town. Her life was governed by a rather demanding mother who brought to bear with regularity the old country adage that children should be seen and not heard. Beyond home and Mother's daily admonitions of what and what not to do, school and the Church gave Phyllis a welcomed reprieve. This diversion was with mother's support as Church was a very important part of her life.

As a young teen, Phyllis joined and sang in the choir at Christ Church and attended, as often as she could, activities of the AYPA – Anglican Young People's Association – where she met and chummed with a young man named Jimmy McLagan. Through the choir she met Mrs. Dorothy Minnie Dymond, a very charming and elegant English woman. Whether it was through her association with Mrs. Dymond or the AYPA, Phyllis soon met Dorothy's son, Donald, and they, Jimmy, Donald and Phyllis, become fast friends.

Donald was born in Bideford, North Devon, England in 1919. Looking to the future and what appeared to be opportunity in Canada, the family emigrated there in 1928. They first lived in London, Ontario, but soon found their way to Chatham, settling there where Donald finished 'lower school' and was working as a printer's assistant at the Mercury Press.

Donald and Phyllis soon became more than just friends and started going steady. At Christmas, 1939, Phyllis discovered, in a small box at the bottom of a package of coal – it was an old custom to give coal as a Christmas gift to those who were naughty and not nice – an elegant, yet simple engagement ring. Donald had a wonderful sense of humor. The question may have been popped, but never the less, Phyllis and Donald became engaged and plans began in earnest for their future together.

THE ENGAGEMENT.
CHRISTMAS, 1939

This Christmas, in addition to being when the ring was discovered surreptitiously buried in a package of coal, is the first time that the two families had come together formally for a meal. Beyond Donald and Phyllis, they had little in common. Being from east of London and North Devon proved distant enough for engaging conversation. Rose, coming from a family of nine and used to preparing large meals had, in the spirit of the season, offered their home for this Christmas gathering. Phyllis had actually insisted, saying that the Dymonds couldn't accommodate both families in their small home. Hence Christmas Day of 1939, with all the customary activities of welcoming handshakes and distant kisses and so nice to see you again regards, had begun. It came with proper English tea, biscuits and, fitting the occasion, glasses of wine and sherry, not to mention the sharing of nominal gifts. It was at 23 Dover Street, Phyllis' home, the home of Billy and Rose Jackson where they had dinner in Rose Jackson fashion with all the seasonal trimmings.

There had always been a little friction between the two families. From a distance, it would appear that family history, about which there was much ado back in merry old England, held little sway in Canada. Who your father was and where he was from did play a major role in the selection of friends and future family members in the upper crust of British society, but not in Canada. In an effort to maintain that aura, a profound sense of pride, misplaced at times in being English and all that is proper, was exuded constantly by Don's mother, Dorothy, in both dress and deportment. However, having immigrated to Canada from England with little but this pride and not having added much to that since arriving, it was a hard pill for the Jacksons to swallow. Never the less, the important people here today were the newly betrothed Donald and Phyllis. Nothing should diminish that, not even a stayed and often aloof, British façade.

Shirley, like the good sister she was, not so happily set the table at mother's direction. With dad in tow like the obedient puppy expressing the occasional, "yes, dear," they placed the right flatware the right way at the side and above each plate after which Shirley poured tomato juice as some toasting was expected. Only the best Blue Willow plates and cornflower glasses would do. The mixed aromas of turkey, ham and Yorkshire pudding saturated the air and affable Rose would soon invite all to share in this season's abundance and blessings.

Billy carefully carved the modest turkey while Phyllis sliced ham at the counter heaping it generously on a platter and placing it on the table. Everyone quickly found their seats. Donald sniffed the air offering loud yummy sounds to the tune of 'Santa Claus is coming to town' at which his mother clucked a stern, "Donald!" He and Phyllis cozied up like love birds on the piano bench, on one side of the table. This is where all future children would sit for birthdays and seasonal repasts. It was what was expected.

Shirley plopped herself down between Phyllis and their dad as Dorothy and Robert filled the chairs directly across from their son and future daughter-in-law. Rose sat in the customary spot of authority opposite end from Billy and quietly motioned in which direction food should be passed. Shirley just shook her head. Conversation slowed as plates were filled, rolls were cut and buttered and all attention focused on the task at hand…eating and enjoying a wonderful Christmas dinner.

"Would you say grace, Donald?" his mother asked curtly smiling at Rose, "before we eat this lovely meal."

Robert W Dymond, Circa 1917

Dorothy M Dymond, Circa 1917

Doreen Brown, cousin. Rose Jackson, 1941

Phyllis E Jackson and father William 'Billy' Jackson, 1919

"Yes, mother," Donald said with a grin, putting down a half-eaten roll, "I will," he continued saying, "sorry, mother, this all smells so good, I just couldn't help myself."

"Don't be impertinent, dear, just go ahead." Shirley rolled her eyes.

Everyone bowed their heads as a thankful silence overtook the table. "For what we are about to receive may the Lord make us truly thankful," Donald stated reverently, then resumed his humming rendition of 'Santa Claus is coming to town'.

With that, Robert quickly took his juice glass in hand offering a toast, "To King and Country. After all, Canada is still part of the British Commonwealth and we should rightly recognize and salute its King." After the toast, and just as quickly so not to be upstaged, Rose took up her glass again and proposed a toast to the future of Phyllis and Donald; that it would be filled with love, laughter and the giggles of children and that the war just declared on Germany by Britain and Canada would remain at a great distance and be short lived.

The hungry group replied like eager, yet obedient children, to both toasts quickly downing their juices. The feast then began in earnest.

Donald, ravenous as usual, was first in and always first out like a starving refugee, leaving little, if any for Mr. Manners. Shirley just played with her food. It was customary in the Dymond household to always leave a little on your plate for Mr. Manners. Scraping the last morsel from the plate of a meal well-enjoyed is hardly necessary and could be considered utterly rude, suggesting the host had not provided enough to eat…an old British mores. We wouldn't want that. Plate heaping and head down, Donald gobbled up every crumb like it was his last after which he sat quietly, but just for a moment. It was his job to eat, Mr. Manners, be damned. He then began to refill his plate.

Shirley, an excited sixteen year old but not at all sure about dinner with the 'snooty Dymond's' as she referred to them, was quietly eager to gaze upon the engagement ring…a simple, yet elegant setting. On a typesetter's income, much is hoped for but little is expected. Phyllis was enthralled.

"Oh, that is nice sis," Shirley whispered, as she gazed directly at Mrs. Dymond, but not to upset the formality of the meal. Shirley was never good at withholding her gaze or her tongue. However, she did garner a 'children should be seen and not heard' stare from Donald's mother, not unlike she would get daily from Rose, her own mother. Well, the English are the English, she thought.

"Can I try it on, sis?" she whispered, rubbing it with her sleeve.

Quickly looking around the table, Phyllis decided discretion might just be the key here and offered a kiss on the cheek and a, "no, not now, but maybe later," response. That seemed to satisfy Shirley, who resumed poking at her food.

"I really enjoyed Reverend Mess' sermon today," Dorothy said enthusiastically. "He made it abundantly clear that this is the season to be thankful for what we do have and not to think too poorly about those that struggle at this time of the year. There were some new faces in the congregation this morning, I noticed, and it seemed he was aiming his comments at them. I really didn't recognize any of these people…did you dear?" she asked calmly, looking at Robert.

Before her husband had a chance to respond, Donald was quick to add a thought.

"C'mon mum, there are always new faces at this time of year and with a war beginning, everybody is looking for a little help. Even the commonest of souls are encouraged to attend church on Christ's birthday. It seems the thing to do and I believe the reverend was thinking as much of us as he was about new people and the war, I guess."

"Well, perhaps," Dorothy said unpretentiously, "and he did speak wonderfully about the wise men and their trip to the baby Jesus." Quickly changing the subject, Dorothy directed her comments to Phyllis. "How long is it now that you two have been dating?"

"Um," Phyllis said looking at a grinning Donald, "about two years, right Ducky?"

Through a mouth full of turkey, Donald replied, "...yes, about that love"

"Donald!" exclaimed Dorothy, "...not with your mouth full!"

His dad just shook his head then brought up a rather delicate subject.

"I suspect the regimental reserves will be busier and somewhat on the alert since war has now been declared. Would you agree, boy?"

"Yes, father, I do agree. In fact, Billy, Jimmie and I have been talking and we are seriously considering joining the active forces. From what I have heard, the numbers in the active militia far outnumber the full-time army complement. Over the next few months there will likely be many boys joining up, and I guess that's why we've been talking about it."

Phyllis continued to eat as though she didn't hear Donald's comment. But she knew as they had talked. This revelation, however, drew a surprised look from his mother, a look that quickly turned gaunt as her face fell. Robert had served with the RAF in Egypt during WWI. He survived, but her memories of those days of fear and hope suddenly brought back pain since forgotten. Robert was taken aback as well and only because he felt that if his son had given serious thought to serve in the forces, with war now declared, that he would have spoken to him first.

A palpable chill overtook the room that all felt. It is Christmas and a time for the joyous celebration of birth and renewal. The New Year was within reach. Talk of lighter, happier things should be the narrative. The gloom of war and all it brings did not belong at this table. However, it was a menacing reality that would slowly and unavoidably seep into the fiber of the country.

"When did you talk about this with your friends?" asked Robert.

"At the AYPA meeting of last week when we were putting together plans for a New Year's dance it came up. I'm not too sure how confident Jimmie was feeling about the idea, but Billy and I were quite serious. Canada is in because Britain is and we felt that whatever happens we didn't want any part of war to end up on our shores here in Canada. It seems like the right thing to do. Is that wrong thinking dad?"

"No, son, it is not. I just thought we might have spoken before you made any decision."

"Well, it's not for sure, dad, but I think we need to be involved in some way."

"I certainly don't approve, Donald," his mother said. "Do you have to join now? Can't you wait until we are well into the new year and see how the conflict goes. Perhaps it will be brief and there will be no need for you to join. I am sure the army has quite enough soldiers for now and with England involved, maybe there will be no need for Canadian assistance."

"Phyllis, how are you feeling about this?" Donald's mother asked, concerned.

"Mother," Donald said rather sharply, "the army doesn't have enough members, but perhaps we should speak of this later. It is Christmas. Shouldn't we be a little more jovial? I do feel I need to do my duty, however, to do what I can do for our country and it is all volunteer. There is no conscription to the service and I expect lots of boys will be lining up to join over the next few months…and, yes, mother, I will wait to see how things go into the new year, then make a decision. Billy Mugridge said he thought it may be a little early, as well, to make that decision. I will wait," he concluded, kissing Phyllis on the cheek. "I just got engaged. We won't be rushing anything, right, love?" he finished, kissing Phyllis again on the cheek.

The need to eat the wonderful meal that Rose had prepared overtook the conversation and scraping forks and sighs of satisfaction prevailed.

"Mrs. Blonde was out in her yard earlier, Mom," Shirley said looking to Rose.

"Was she?" Rose asked. "She has been a little under the weather recently. It is good to see her out and about a bit."

"Maybe we should send her over a plate of food later," Shirley added. "She probably doesn't cook much for herself. I don't think you do that much when you are alone all the time... and sick too."

"Perhaps you should run over a little later, Shirley, and ask." Rose suggested.

"Okay, mom," Shirley replied.

"Phyllis," Rose asked, "will you put the pudding sauce on to heat? I am sure we will be having dessert soon...and the kettle, too please, for tea?"

Without saying a word, Phyllis got up, went to the stove and slid the sauce pot onto the heated part of the stove and filled the kettle.

"Boy," Robert asked. "Who did you say has been talking about joining?"

"Jimmie McClagan and Billy Mugridge, dad. Maybe some other fellows too."

"What is the general thinking?" his dad continued.

"It seems we are at war, father. It has been all over the papers and on the radio. Canadians may be slow to act and maybe a little reluctant, but there will be much more conversation in the new year, I'm sure. Although Canada has been there before, and England too, dad, many boys will be joining. They feel it's their duty. There has been lots of talk at the armory and they have started to put up posters to get people to join."

"You know the history, dad," Donald continued excitedly. "Canada followed Britain in last time and they are doing it again. I don't know what Heir Hitler's big plan is, but he is spreading into countries around him, I'm sure England is on his radar and Canada may be on his list too. I don't know about the United States, they're not saying much."

"I thought we weren't going to talk about this, Donald? "Mother asked.

"Yes, sorry, mother, guess I got a little carried away. Sorry to you too, dad. Let's just eat shall we. I'm sure there will be lots of talk later."

"So," asked Rose, "have you two set a wedding date?"

Phyllis and Donald looked at each other. "Not really," Phyllis said, "we just got engaged, Mom, maybe we need a little more time."

"I'd like a fall wedding," Donald added, "and we have talked a bit about that. Not having been with the Press that long, waiting until next fall does give me time to save some money…and what's the rush anyway, we have the rest of our lives."

"Maybe not with a war starting," Shirley quietly commented.

Everyone just stared at Shirley. "Right, not now, sorry," she said apologetically.

The meal continued as did conversation about Robert's travels on his sales route for Sulman's stationery, Billy's work for Chatham's public works and its current efforts patching holes in the road on Grand Ave West, and the general state of the economy. Phyllis queried as to whether the river was frozen sufficiently for skating which prompted Dorothy to say that she didn't think the river was safe at any time for skating and that she shouldn't think anyone should be on it. Donald quickly informed his mother that ice taxis run people along the river to the Bay all the time and if that is the case it should certainly be safe for skating.

As bellies filled and conversation diminished, Rose made a pot of tea and asked who would like dessert, which was her homemade Christmas pudding and hot sauce. Out of respect, everyone said yes, "but just a little please," as the main course was wonderful yet very filling. After dessert was consumed, Rose shooed everyone but the girls to the front room for tea and for those who smoked, a quiet cigarette with tea. The girls knew full-well their after-dinner role… scrape and stack plates for washing.

Robert and Billy relaxed over tea and a cigarette, taking up again discussion about local politics and Canada's involvement in the war. Dorothy, much to Rose's surprise said she would help with kitchen cleanup and Donald and Phyllis quietly grabbed their coats and slipped out for a walk in the snow. They had much to talk about.

Walking down the driveway, Phyllis took out two smokes and lit them both while Donald sang his compilation of carols.

"You'd better watch out, you better not cry, you better not pout, I'm telling you why…cause sleigh bells ring are you listening…it's the first noel and the snow is glistening…as the herald angels sing on this silent night."

"That's really not how they go, Duck, you know," Phyllis laughed.

"You almost made a rhyme love," Donald laughed back.

At the end of the drive Donald stopped. "Boy, your mum sure puts on a good spread. Okay, Phyl, which way?"

"Well, I'd like to see if the river is really frozen enough for skating. We can slip down by the bridge."

"Okay, my dear," Donald agreed, "to the bridge it is."

Snow had been lightly falling throughout the day and collecting evenly most everywhere creating a perfect

Christmas scene in all directions. Their breath froze into mist as they exhaled while crossing a now quiet Dover Street. There was not a car to be seen, nor a sound to be heard, only the snow crunching noisily beneath their feet. It was Christmas. All good people were home with family.

The sun had sunk from the sky some time ago and what little light remained from the street lamps gently flickered like a candle flame through the falling flakes. The Thames River lay just around the corner of the British Leaf Tobacco company, which loomed its three floors over the face of 23 Dover Street. Down the Thames Valley road to the left and just past the old asphalt plant that sat dormant beside the river, was their path. Five minutes and they would be there.

"The neighborhood kids come this way all the time," Phyllis said as she slid through the snow, "as I used to, as well."

"I'll bet Shirley has coaxed a few of the local boys down for a little show and tell," said Donald with a dirty grin. Phyllis just punched him in the arm with a tsk, tsk, tsk! "Don't talk that way about my little sister, my good sir. She is a nice girl."

"As pure as this driven snow," Donald added.

"Well," Phyllis continued somewhat sarcastically, "I don't know about that."

"Okay, down to business," Donald declared grabbing her arm and pulling her close. "Is that what we want to do, have our wedding in the fall?"

"We would be able to plan it better that far out and save a little more money, as you said." Phyllis responded. "And you'll have more time to think about enlisting full time," a comment she finished through a sad face.

As they grew close to the river's edge, as close as they dared without the fear of sliding down the snow covered bank, Donald stopped and butted his smoke in the snow. It is Christmas Eve. No one was on the river. However, there were signs of a skating rink in process with a small area cleared away about fifteen feet out. Two shovels stood in a pile of cleared snow as silent sentinels on duty to protect that location.

Winters had been fiercely cold these past few years, cold enough for the river to easily freeze solid. Many people enjoyed its use, along with a couple of taxis with chains on their rear wheels that would whisk people out to Mitchell's Bay for more adventurous skating and ice fishing. It was a picture-perfect winter setting and a night to enjoy a romantic walk with serious talk about the future. Staring at the river and the half-started skating rink, Phyllis now had an answer. "Guess the river is frozen solid enough for skating, eh Ducky?"

Donald was deep in thought. He had really just started working full-time for the Mercury Press. It would be prudent to hold off setting a wedding date until they knew how well he could save some money as Phyllis was not employed and when, or if, he would join the active forces. Fellows he talked with at work, and Billy and Jimmie, seemed to think that there should be a special timing for their enlisting. He certainly got the impression that there was a lot of talk by a lot of people and a momentum was building toward a mass enlisting by a lot of boys.

There is still a feeling of loyalty to Britain rushing through the veins of the larger Canadian public, plus the view of Hitler and what he now appears to be up to is not very good. Those fellows Donald has spoken with display a strong sense of duty to country and believe that joining the full-time forces was the correct thing to do.

He thought about Mom and Dad. He thought about fighting on the shores of Canada which really frightened him. He thought about Phyllis and a future complete with children. He thought about his friends and his not wanting to let them down if they enlisted and he didn't. He thought about Phyllis, again. He then thought about himself and reasoned somewhat out loud saying, "I just turned twenty. I have my whole life ahead of me. Joining the army with the potential of going to war? Is that really what I should be doing?"

"You did say that quietly, Ducky, but I did hear you and I feel the same. I don't know what you should do. This is all new to me. I don't know what joining means or where you'll be. I just want us to be together. Guess we'll just have to wait and see."

As the world shuddered in disbelief, Hitler, a scant three months earlier, had begun his reign of terror to rule Europe, and marched boldly into Poland. Donald had been active in the local militia for quite some time, and fearing for the future; his and Phyllis' future; decided to join the Canadian Active Forces and signed up on July 26, 1940. Donald was the seventh man to enlist with the Kent Regiment in Chatham which at that time was celebrating two years as an active service unit and was seeking to expand its ranks for the looming conflict. It was eventually to become of a greater force: the Algonquin Regiment. The following month, on Labor Day, Monday, September 2, Donald and Phyllis were married at Christ Church.

The paper reported:

Christ Church was the scene of another pretty military wedding at two-thirty o'clock on Monday afternoon when Phyllis Ethel Jackson, daughter of Mr. and Mrs. W. Jackson, became the bride of Corporal Donald William Dymond of the Kent Regiment C.A.S.F., only son of Mr. and Mrs. Robert W. Dymond of this city. White and pink gladioli formed an artistic floral setting for the wedding ceremony which was performed by the rector, Rev. Roy D. Mess. The bride's father gave her hand in marriage and Mrs. Cyril Luff played the wedding music.

The bride was lovely in a gown of pink net over satin with pink silk turban and bouquet of cream roses. The groom was in his military best. Her sister, Shirley Jackson, attending as bridesmaid, wore turquoise taffeta with picture hat and carried a bouquet of pink snapdragons.

William Mugridge, Donald W Dymond, Phyllis E Dymond, sister Shirley Jackson, September 2, 1940.

How could it be any better? After a short honeymoon to Niagara Falls and Toronto, they settled at his parent's home in Chatham before Donald left for training.

HOW IT MIGHT HAVE BEEN

"I know we've talked about this, Ducky," Phyllis said softly, "but do we really have to live at your place after the honeymoon? Your mom doesn't think I'm good enough for you, I know that. It will just be so hard: it will…and your room is so small and I know it is not much better at my house, but please…"

"Sweetheart," Don quickly assured her, "do not pay mother any mind. She really doesn't feel that way. I think all moms are like that. It just seems like she doesn't like you. Besides, dad loves you…it will be all right." With that, Don smiled, hugged Phyllis and kissed her…a kiss that did linger.

Two weeks to the wedding and this wasn't the first discussion about Don's mother and where they would live after their honeymoon. It had always been a bit of a sore point with Phyllis as she was convinced that Dorothy Minnie Dymond of North Devon, England felt that her son could do so much better than the daughter of a housekeeper and a common laborer. It would not be the last words.

September, 2 1940. Christ Church, 2:30 pm.

It was a simple wedding. Its meaning far outweighed the opulence, certainly not part of this ceremony, which too often overshadows such unions of love and devotion. The "I will" and "till death us do part" were far too significant here, as were the military overtones with Donald and his best man, William Mugridge, in full uniform. Beside all that, Donald and Phyllis were truly in love.

Cyril Luff, another member of the Kent Regiment and in full dress, acted as usher. His wife, Nellie, organist for the ceremony and close friend, sat proudly at the organ. She was playing for the radiant bride who was tightly hugging the arm of her father, Billy Jackson, as they walked down the aisle. Shirley, the sister and uninspired bridesmaid, followed quietly toward where the rector, Roy D. Mess, waited with a jubilantly impatient Donald for the bride's arrival. This was what Phyllis wanted, what she always wanted, what she had waited in earnest for over the past year.

Family and friends from both sides filled the front pews of the church, flanked by a core of Don's regimental boys-in-arms, all grinning countenances aside, in freshly pressed uniforms and gleaming boots. Their mothers would be proud.

Standing before the altar Don took the hand of Phyllis and together, anxiously, solemnly, they faced the rector. The organ silenced its welcome; the customary coughs and shifting in the pews settled as Reverend Mess smiled warmly, raised his face to the congregation, and began the long awaited service.

"The grace of our Lord Jesus Christ, the love of God and the fellowship of the Holy Spirit be with you."

"And also with you," came the traditional reply.

"God is love, and those who live in love live in God and God lives in them," he continued and with that, offered a long, warm fatherly gaze at these two young souls, who he had known for some time, as both were active members of the Church's, Anglican Young People's Association, and Phyllis a devout member of the choir. He, too, wondered where the years had gone, as yet, again, he was sending two young, and happily anxious spirits out into the world, together, to make a life in the very midst of trying times.

He continued, "In the presence of God, Father, Son and Holy Spirit, we have come together to witness the marriage of Donald and Phyllis, to pray for God's blessing on them, to share their joy and to celebrate their love.

Marriage is a gift of God in creation through which husband and wife may know the grace of God. It is given that as man and woman grow together in love and trust, they shall be united in one another, body and mind, as Christ is united with his bride, the Church. Marriage is a way of life made holy by God, and blessed by the presence of our Lord Jesus Christ with those celebrating a wedding at Cana in Galilee. Marriage is a sign of unity and loyalty which all should uphold and honor."

The good Reverend was now in sermon mode.

"It enriches society and strengthens community. No one should enter into it lightly or selfishly but reverently and responsibly in the sight of almighty God.

Donald and Phyllis are now to enter this way of life. They will each give their consent to the other and make solemn vows, and in token of this will each give and receive a ring. We pray with them that the Holy Spirit will guide and strengthen them, that they may fulfil God's purpose for the whole of their earthly life together."

A few expected giggles trickled through the uniformed section of the congregation... mostly boys and childhood friends of Donald's. These were quickly quelled with a brief and understanding gaze by Reverend Mess. Boys will be boys he no doubt thought. He continued once again focusing his attention to the congregation of family and friends.

"First, I am required to ask anyone present who knows a reason why these persons may not lawfully marry, to declare it now," he spoke in official tones followed with the customary and momentary glance through the crowd, then with an accepting smile, back to the patient couple.

"The vows you are about to take are to be made in the presence of God, who is judge of all and knows all the secrets of our hearts; therefore if either of you knows a reason why you may not lawfully marry, you must declare it now."

Hearing the expected silence, he carries on directing his attention to Donald.

"Donald, will you take Phyllis to be your wife? Will you love her, comfort her, honor and protect her, and, forsaking all others, be faithful to her as long as you both shall live?"

"I will," an assured yet nervous Donald replies.

Now smiling at Phyllis, "Phyllis, will you take Donald to be your husband? Will you love him, comfort him, honor and protect him, and, forsaking all others, be faithful to him as long as you both shall live?"

"I will," Phyllis replies smiling at Donald through welling eyes.

Shifting his attention to the congregation, the reverend asks. "Will you, the families and friends of Donald and Phyllis, support and uphold them in their marriage now and in the years to come?"

"We will," was the confident response.

"Let us pray," Reverend Mess invited, raising his arms openly.

"God our Father, from the beginning you have blessed creation with abundant life. Pour out your blessings upon Donald and Phyllis that they may be joined in mutual love and companionship, in holiness and commitment to each other.

We ask this through our Lord Jesus Christ, your Son, who is alive and reigns with you, in the unity of the Holy Spirit, one God, now and forever."

"Amen," a comforting response from all.

Turning again to the wedding couple, Reverend Mess introduces the vows.

"Donald and Phyllis, I now invite you to join hands and make your vows, in the presence of God and his people." He asks that they face each other and that Donald take Phyllis' hand.

"Donald, please repeat after me." Which Donald does…

"I, Donald William Dymond, take you, Phyllis Ethyl Jackson, to be my wife, to have and to hold from this day forward; for better, for worse, for richer, for poorer, in sickness and in health, to love and to cherish, till death us do part; according to God's holy law. In the presence of God I make this vow."

They unclasp hands and Phyllis then takes Donald's hand nervously smiling at him.

"I, Phyllis Ethyl Jackson, take you, Donald William Dymond, to be my husband, to have and to hold from this day forward; for better, for worse, for richer, for poorer, in sickness and in health, to love and to cherish, till death us do part; according to God's holy law. In the presence of God I make this vow."

…Donald and Phyllis loose hands as the reverend received the rings.

"Heavenly Father," he implored, "by your blessing let these rings be to Donald and Phyllis a symbol of unending love and faithfulness, to remind them of the vow and covenant which they have made this day through Jesus Christ our Lord."

Donald places the ring on Phyllis' finger and holding it there says...

"Phyllis, I give you this ring as a sign of our marriage. With my body I honor you, all that I am I give to you, and all that I have I share with you, within the love of God, Father, Son and Holy Spirit."

Phyllis places the ring on Donald's finger and holding it there repeats...

"Donald, I give you this ring as a sign of our marriage. With my body I honor you, all that I am I give you, and all that I have I share with you, within the love of God, Father, Son and Holy Spirit."

The reverend turns and addresses the congregation...

"In the presence of God, and before this congregation, Donald and Phyllis have given their consent and made their marriage vows to each other. They have declared their marriage by the joining of hands and by the giving and receiving of rings. I therefore proclaim that they are husband and wife. Those whom God has joined together let no one put asunder."

Turning to Donald and Phyllis, Reverend Mess concludes the ceremony with a blessing.

"God the Father, God the Son, God the Holy Spirit, bless, preserve and keep you; Lord mercifully grant you the riches of his grace, that you may please him both in body and soul, and, living together in faith and love, may receive the blessings of eternal life."

There were further squirmings, like anxious children awaiting recess, and signs of impatience brewing in the congregation as the bride and groom kissed, like a first kiss, then retired from the main body of the Church to complete the registration of the marriage. As they left the reverend concluded the event.

"Momentarily, Mr. and Mrs. Dymond will return and proceed back up the aisle and out the main door," informed a very animated Reverend Mess. "Please cheer and congratulate them as you see fit, however, if it is your need to throw confetti, please do so outside the building as it displeases the cleaning staff greatly who have to rescue those bits of paper, to the garbage, from the various nooks and crannies of the Church. Also, Rose and William Jackson," gesturing to the front row of pews, "parents of the bride, will be holding the reception a little later in their home at 23 Dover Street, at five pm I am told. Most of you will likely know where that is. A light lunch will be provided, courtesy of Mr. and Mrs. Jackson, and you will be able to further congratulate Donald and Phyllis before they depart on their honeymoon, which I believe will include visits to both Niagara Falls and Toronto. Thank you all for attending on this occasion. May God bless you and keep you."

It wasn't long before a truly blushing bride and an anxious groom appeared from the side room and walked proudly, as though on a cloud, up the aisle to the main door where, on exiting, they were well received with cheers, hugs, whistles and more than enough confetti. Pictures were taken and they were swiftly led to the groomsman's awaiting car.

However supportive Army Command was of having enlisted men marry, chances are that a leave of three or four days was all that had been approved. Donald volunteered for service as conscription had not yet arrived for this war and he was just a corporal. A higher rank may have garnered him a longer honeymoon leave.

By five that evening the reception was well underway at the Jackson's of Dover Street. Rose had baked specifically for this event: rolls, butter tarts and apple pie, and all the best Sunday china and flatware flattered the kitchen table. Shirley passed out hors d'oeuvres to a hungry entourage and toasts were given to the newlyweds with this year's home-made wine. Cold beer could be found in the ice box and Rose's canned pickles and onions added a touch of class and flavor to the ham sandwiches and potato salad, this item specially prepared by Shirley. Some speeches were made later in the evening, after Phyllis and Donald left, by those boys loosened by the uninhibiting nature of cold beer and wine. Rose and Billy were very happy for their daughter and proud to have Donald as a part of their family.

Tickets for the evening train to Niagara Falls had been purchased and given as a wedding gift to the happy couple by Mr. Jon Koning of the Mercury Press, for whom Donald had worked as a type setter. Train time was 5:50 that evening and all knew that CPR runs on schedule and that getting there on time was imperative and the responsibility of Corporal Billy Mugridge, Don's best man and good friend.

Following all the appropriate pleasantries, toasts, rushed speeches and hugs for special friends and family, it was off to the train station for the new Mr. and Mrs. Dymond. Don's father, Robert, had agreed, at the last minute, to drive them. The best man had consumed one too many beers. Robert was adamant that they leave immediately in order to not miss the train…the first official event together in the couple's new life. Dorothy Dymond, Don's mother, unexpectedly hugged Phyllis closely as though she was an old friend found, and sincerely welcomed her to the family. That got an I-told-you-so smile from Donald and a look of stunned surprise from Phyllis. But it was all good and lent itself firmly to the foundation for the new lives of Donald and Phyllis.

The train was on time. They were on time, barely, and off to a new adventure. Changing trains was required in London, which went smoothly, and they were on to a late arrival in Niagara Falls as the newly minted Mr. and Mrs. Donald William Dymond.

Donald's leave ended at midnight on the fifth at which time he needed to report back to London's Wolseley Barracks for duty. This played on their minds somewhat, certainly Phyllis', as she knew their time together would be short and they had to make the best of it. They were both anxious to see the falls as honeymooners and the CNE (Canadian National Exhibition) in Toronto which is held annually during the latter part of August and into September…a lot to do and with so little time.

THE HONEYMOON

"Wouldn't it have been nice to have a berth on this train and stay in it tonight, you know, sleep here, sweetie," Phyllis said through a devilish grin. "It would be so romantic... hmm, sex on a train for our honeymoon. Don't you think so, Ducky?" she said, nibbling at Donald's ear.

"A berth: who needs a berth?" Donald growled in a whisper, "George is up for the task right now...right here in this window-seat my darling," he said, looking around at the lifeless, empty car. "No one will even know. It is all but shadows in every corner. We can be quite quiet, right? Move to the sounds of the clicking rails. We've been quiet before at both my and your place...remember?" he said slyly. "No one will ever know...oh yeah, in dad's car, in the drive too.... hmm? And, did you pack some smokes?"

Phyllis looked about anxiously, cheeks flushed with the thought of the cookie taken behind mother's back, almost embarrassed like they would be cheating or stealing something that wasn't yet fully theirs...maybe even kicked off the train if discovered. She turned and gently pushed her lips to his. This kiss was forever.

"...and yes, Forgetful," she said, "I did pack some smokes."

They cuddled and in the window watched the reflection the world of trees, hills and distant lights of sleepy communities created on passing. It was finally just them. How could it be any better?

Niagara Falls: home of the historic honeymoon. Don and Phyl stayed at a quaint little inn discovered just off the main street and only six blocks from the falls. It was late when they checked in and they were tired, but excited that it was finally over, the waiting that is, and they could now focus on their future. Despite the war, which was still very much in the distance, thinking and talking about a home and kids was very much in vogue.

After a brief settling in, which was easy as they each brought minimal clothing, a few passionate kisses were exchanged and the newlyweds, albeit tired, were hungry, not ready for bed, and decided on an evening walk.

The night was warm but that did not keep them from a comforting, arm-in-arm stroll like old friends. In the distance they thought they could hear a muffled roar of the falls itself. The occasional car horn and the whir of tires drifted their way on a warm late summer's breeze. Just up ahead they heard Italian music, which on following the sound, brought them to a small Italian bistro. Grinning at each other like children, they nodded their heads in unison and went in. A glass of wine, fresh, warm bread with spaghetti and meatballs did the trick. They lingered, laughed, hugged and kissed. Phyllis shed a few emotional tears, kissed away by Donald, but most of all they were finally together as one and the future was theirs.

Now that they were in one of the most popular, undisputed honeymoon destinations in the West, they agreed that not seeing the falls at night would be a crime. After Donald paid the check they left the restaurant hand-in-hand and turned toward the distant roar heard earlier. Within a few short moments they were there. They wandered around the civic park areas, stood by the rails near the falls, watched the mist rise from the cascading waters shimmering through the spots lights and felt it collect on their faces like the morning's dew. They kissed and held each other tightly. There were no words spoken, just the welcomed and palpable silence of their being together.

An overwhelming sense of comfort and security swept over Phyllis like a warm blanket. She had always felt this way when with Donald but somehow now it felt for sure, like it came with a written guarantee, irrevocable and forever.

Back in the room they undressed each other slowly, deliberately. The days of rushed passion were history. Sharing the heat of their eager bodies, they held each other tightly, kissed like it was their last, made the most wonderful love ever and soon fell asleep as one. Tomorrow will be another day.

Morning passed uninhibited by thoughts of what may be. It was the now that filled their every moment. They languished over coffee, tea, fresh preserves on warm toast, steeped in the sanctity of their real, first morning together. They had discovered a little café just behind the inn of the first night. It was all so romantic.

The rest of the day was filled wandering the streets and shops of the falls: not a moment was squandered. They were so engrossed in talks of their hopes and plans for tomorrow and beyond that, they found themselves rushing to catch the evening train to Toronto.

Finding a hotel of reasonable rate and both convenient to the west end train station and the CNE grounds was their challenge on arrival. On recommendation of a taxi driver, they found a small inn near the lakeshore that did the trick. By this time it was night and knowing the length and breadth of the CNE exposition decided that venturing there might best be left till morning.

"Frank Sinatra is performing at the Ex this year, you know darling," Donald said as they prepared for bed.

"No, he is not!" Phyllis replied quickly, knowing that Donald was always fooling with her.

"I'm sorry, my dear, but he most certainly is. It was in the London paper. Why, my love… don't you read?"

Phyllis tackled Donald and threw him onto the bed and beat him about the head with a pillow, shouting, "You stinker, why didn't you tell me! You're mean!" she scolded.

"I planned no surprises for our trip, love…I just thought you would have known."

"Well, smarty-pants, I didn't." Then with a sly smile she asks, "…will we get to see him tomorrow?"

"Hope so," Donald replied. "Not sure what the show-times are or exactly where he is playing, but we will find that out in the morning."

The CNE did not open till ten o'clock daily, so there was no rush to get there early, Donald had said. The long walk to the main Dufferin Gates would be good for them on a brisk, fall morning. Without breakfast, they struck out at 9 am and arrived at the gates fifteen minutes ahead of their official opening.

"A coffee and a warm bun would be nice," Donald said, "… and I am sure we will be able to get that once we get inside."

"That will do me just fine," Phyllis added, "and I am sure that we will be able to get cotton candy somewhere in there, too, as you can't go to any circus or carnival without having cotton-candy. It's a rule….right, Ducky?"

Donald just laughed as they checked out the price of admission. Soon the gates opened and in they went with a bounce in their step.

The Canadian National Exhibition, Toronto, Canada, touted as the largest exposition of its kind in North America has been around since 1879. Its beginnings were in support of new technologies and agriculture. Today, as in 1940, it is considerably more than that. The population of Canada in 1940 was about eleven million people, and most would file through the symbolic Dufferin Gates over the almost three weeks of its annual run. Second only to the thrill of their honeymoon, Donald and Phyllis are enthralled with it all and excited to take in as much of the displays, rides and shows as they could in one full day including taking 'snaps' for everyone back home.

Conklin Shows, one of the leading organizers behind the CNE were advertising this year's newest product…ice cream waffles something they both wanted in addition to seeing Mr. Sinatra live.

They walked, looked, read, ate, witnessed the unveiling of new technologies, took snaps, went on a couple of rides and searched out where Frank S would be performing until their feet could take no more. The high point of this honeymoon was, in fact, that it was a honeymoon, and Donald and Phyllis were now happily Mr. and Mrs. Dymond. That was all they cared about and spending as much time together as possible before Don was back to duty. This ended up being the best thing as Mr. Sinatra was not performing until September 5th, the day that Don needed to be back in the barracks in London. While they were sorely disappointed in missing the event, these three days together were to be the best, happiest days of their life so far, and they would cherish them forever…and they would have snaps too.

Dusk and weariness set in (as old friends) about the same time. Their thoughts now were of the inn, their bed, each other's arms and sleep, indeed of the whole three days and not of what returning home offers. Donald will be gone and not sure when they will see each other again.

"Wow! What a day," Phyllis exclaimed through a yawn. "My dogs are barking...they are ready to take a nap. I think we must have walked one-hundred miles sweetie...at least... should have brought different, better, shoes. I can hear that little bed calling us. Oh boy"

"I expect I'll be doing a lot of this over the next few months," Donald explained,"...walking, that is. I think that when they say join the army and see the world on your belly, that's because your feet, after a few months, just can't take it any longer."

Donald grew quiet for a moment as he lit a cigarette and shared it with Phyllis. He seemed to slow their pace of walk back to the inn: more of a shuffle than a walk.

"I know why I joined my love, you know the army, but after today, after this whole week, I don't want to go back. Is that a bad thing for me to feel, darling? I mean, I did volunteer. I can just hear dad if I mentioned feeling this way to him," shaking his head as they walked.

Phyllis said nothing, she just held tight to Don's arm. The walk back to the inn was quiet, yet comfortable.

HEADING TO OUR NEW HOME

Riding the rails, as Don called it, was something that Phyllis liked. It is romantic, but she had done little of it. Her family rarely travelled. Saving your pennies and putting food on the table fit mother's philosophy much better. Donald has had a few rides since joining the active forces, but only enjoyed it when he was going home. Today they were together, married, and going home. Although words were exchanged about where they were to live home would be temporarily at his folk's house, in his room, in the home of mammie and pappy as Phyllis would come to call Don's folks.

As the sun set red and inviting before them, they laughed, talked and planned their future over the sound of clicking rails, haunting whistles and quick stops at the many little towns, all part of the fullness of the event. The three or so hours passed unnoticed as Phyllis' only thoughts were of creating a life together. For all her life it seemed she had longed to be out of the home of, and away from, the mother who dominated her. Her father, unfortunately, was merely a bystander in most discussions. Thinking and doing on your own was frowned upon by mother and speaking out most often warranted a slap. Shirley, Phyllis' younger sister, fought constantly with their mother but managed to get her own way despite being admonished by dad, who most often just threw up his hands. She received the odd slap on the side of the head from mother, but Shirley went her way. Phyllis just could not do this. It was not part of her make up, so she just towed the line like a leashed puppy. It was easier.

William Mugridge, Don's groomsman, was waiting at the train station to pick them up. He was quick to apologize for not being up to the task of getting them to the train after the reception. Don just punched him in the arm and laughed. That's what good friends did. William smiled as he opened the car door and invited his charges into the back seat. He grabbed their shared suitcase, popped it into the trunk and off they went to the home of Don's parents up on Thames Street...the new, temporary, home of Mr. and Mrs. Dymond.

"So, what side of the bed do I sleep on?" Phyllis quietly queried as she whispered, "I love you Ducky," in Don's ear.

"Hmm, not sure," Don replied, "Maybe in the middle where you can't get away from me and George. You know how anxious he will be to settle in, if you get my drift."

"I like the sound of that," Phyllis sighed. "...can hardly wait," as she cuddled in the back seat.

The Dymond family home would be hers for the foreseeable future. She felt strongly that she and Don's mom, mammie, could find common ground, which was her son. Pappy was no problem. They had always got along famously, even to the point where he was teaching her to drive and giving her tennis lessons. A warm, trusting relationship was being built and that would stand for much in the coming years of separation, fear, hope and the raising of two children.

Both William Mugridge and Don had received leave through to midnight on September 5th. Donald and Phyllis had very little time left together now before he had to leave for London. Another friend and new recruit unable to get a leave for the ceremony had reluctantly given his car to William for the trip to and from the wedding. This would get William and Donald back to London a little later and in time for their midnight curfew.

The newly minted couple was warmly welcomed into their new, temporary, home with firm hugs and kisses...and a cup of hot English tea with biscuits. Phyllis, not a tea drinker, patiently dipped biscuits till her cup was empty and refused a second saying that she was done-in and that she and Don should get unpacked and him ready for his trip back to the barracks.

An intimate few minutes were almost impossible to find, but the newlyweds, undaunted by a prying parent, sought intimacy as quietly as possible in the privacy of their own room and on a three-quarter bed, just next to the bedroom of mom and dad. This required skill and cunning the likes of which can always be found by a young, anxious couple with little time to spare and much love to share. Who knows when they will see each other again? But it was not to be. Like a drill sergeant, William gave the order that they be on the road within the half-hour.

Avoiding the obvious, they sauntered arm-in-arm to the awaiting car for the boy's trip back to the barracks, Phyllis, melancholy and clinging, shed tears of silence as they walked.

Don, the usual life of the party, dismayed, yet resigned, held tightly Phyllis' hand as they strode. Mom, as moms will always be, expressed a mother's uneasiness. Her son was leaving…again. She had already lost one child, a daughter, to the new world. Losing her son would be unthinkable. Dad, proud as ever and as pragmatic as always, wore a stoic façade and it would still be, as always, ship-shape and Bristol fashion…British to the core…stiff upper lip. William, driver for the evening, was simply anxious to be on their way. He knew how costly the emotions of leaving were and sought to allay whatever pain he could with a quick exit. Sadly, that did not work. Hugs, kisses and promises to write, call, and take care wore on. For William this was just too much. After more than just a few minutes, he jumped into the car, started it and slowly pulled away from the curb. This was all that was needed. Don got in and away they drove.

Knowing full-well the complicated nature of leaving, Phyllis had already confirmed a visit to the barracks in London for the following week and they would be discussing the very possibility of her finding accommodation in London, for whatever period of time could be worked out, to be near the love of her life.

DETAILS

Donald W Dymond, 1942

On January 16, 1941, hundreds of other local boys, many in their teens, donned their full militia dress, as Donald had - helmets, back-packs and weapons - and marched to the cheers and victory wishes of thousands from Chatham's Tecumseh Park to the CPR train station from which they embarked for London's Wolseley Barracks. Donald had left for training earlier in the month, briefly stationed in Kingston, hoping for a weekend soon to visit his beloved and expecting to move back to the barracks in London.

As often as she could, Phyllis would stay in London near the barracks in order to be as close to the love of her life as she could. Donald's training and responsibilities took him from one Canadian coast to the other and into Quebec for focused officer studies.

Donald was able to obtain furlough on a few occasions to visit his bride at home, and once when his father, Robert, was in a serious car accident in the fall of 1941. On one of those visits, as Phyllis would one day say, "I was caught with Margo" and on February 1/1942, their first child, a girl, was born. They and their families were thrilled and Donald became a very proud father. At this time, Phyllis moved back to her parent's home where they had created an apartment for her and Margo.

In June of 1943, as Donald's training continued and as he moved up through the ranks to Lieutenant, he and thousands of other soldiers boarded a ship in Windsor, Nova Scotia, and embarked for England to finalize their training before hitting the war's front in France. Donald was able to gain his last furlough earlier in the year before sailing to England, at which time, Phyllis again said that she was "caught, this time, with Michael" and their second child, a son, was born on November 15, 1943. Their family was now complete. Sadly, Donald would never hold this child.

Donald's training continued intensely in England and his love for Phyllis continued through many letters. In July the following year, 1944, he and his Company embarked for the French shores to begin their war effort. Their company fought bravely through France, Belgium, and Holland and finally into Germany. The letters continued.

On April 30, 1945, one week before victory was sounded in Europe, and at the rank of Captain, Donald was killed in action. He saw and held Margo, but was never to gaze into the eyes of his son, Michael. Phyllis and their families were shattered. Nothing would be the same.

Donald and Phyllis Dymond, 1943

Wars and undying love seem to go hand in hand. However tragic both can be, humanity cannot seem to avoid one and survive without the other. And so it goes.

War really played no part in the tragic love of Romeo and Juliet, but warring families can offer the same sense of isolation and hopelessness. However, undaunted determination kept two 'star-crossed' lovers yearning for passion's unending kiss.

Dr. Zhivago, a married and respected doctor, in the uncertainty of Russia's Revolution discovered love and endured the divisive politics of class in his quest for the beguiling Lara.

And who can forget Ric and Ilsa…hearts torn apart by the senseless ravages of war and another love's devotion. Love got in love's way.

Phyllis and Donald are none of these, yet love recognizes no political, religious or class barriers and will find a way… in spite of family rejections, political allegiances and the horrors of war. Through the years and over an ocean's daunting distance, their passion for each other was buoyed and sustained by true love; dreams of a future together and a family, only to be silenced by the devastation of that war's dying hours.

Fighting is part of the nature of the beast mankind. If we feel threatened and in dire peril struggling to acquire what we need and protect what we have, when all else fails we will fight. Right and wrong do fit comfortably into that notion.

However, want and avarice, when left unchecked will slip in and aggressive we will become. Like Hitler, we will simply want to take. Sadly, it is another part of mankind.

War got what it needed. Donald and Phyllis did not.

Donald was a simple, loving soul who wanted a simple life: home, wife and family. Right and wrong were easy for him. War anywhere was wrong and certainly on his shore. Right was to fight to keep that from happening.

LETTERS FROM 1941

Donald and Phyllis had been married and together just four months. This is the first time they have been apart. Donald's letters are somewhat light and humorous as they were newlyweds and still checking each other out. From Kingston through London - marching and a bout with the measles - Hamilton, Halifax to Niagara. Life and love fill the letters.

4:20 p.m. Wed, Jan. 5, 1941

My Dear Phyllis:

Well Ducky, another day is well under way & my rash is gone. I still have a cough, but I guess it will be gone before long.

How are you making out sweetheart, hope you are happy. I haven't heard from you yet, I hope to soon.

Capt. Foex was out here a few minutes ago, he didn't say anything much.

Gord Chatterton was out in the hall this afternoon & I was talking to him for a while.

There are about 12 of us out here from the Kents.

I learned how to play cribbage.

We couldn't figure out anything to do this afternoon, then I thought of filling my mess-tin with paper & using it for a ball, so we did & had a good time until Pte. St. John threw it crooked & hit a pop-bottle on my table which hit my drinking glass & broke it to pieces, some fun!

By the way, we have a little blond day nurse here, & an elderly one by night. Two men by day and one by night.

I was really surprised to see dad looking in the window yesterday.

Well Darling, how have you been sleeping this week. Hope you will be rested up when I get home. I should be well rested myself, oh boy!

Well, Sweetheart, I'm afraid my letters this week have been a little uninteresting, but there doesn't seem anything to talk about.

Look after yourself dear, give my love to mum and dad, God bless you dear & keep happy.

So-long dear, from your ever loving husband.

XXXXXX   Don.

Jan. 15/1941, C.S.A.C.T. A.P.
Kingston, Ont.

My Darling Wife:

Please excuse the paper Darling, but I am out of letter paper.

The boys are playing with a French Safe here, pulling it over the end of a broom; some fun, ay kid?

I suppose you will have my letter telling you that I must return to London. But I'm going to do my darndest to get home for the weekend. I don't know what I will do if I have to stay away from you much longer. I'm getting to miss you more and more, & every time I'm still, I keep getting warmer; you know what I mean.

ᚦ Ducky ᚦ

So Shirley is in the family way. I guess that doesn't make you feel so good, kid; but never mind, you've got a clean slate. Even if we did things before we were married, they weren't really wrong, it was love that brought <u>us</u> together, but I don't think it was love in her case. Anyway, let's not worry about it, she will get along some way. We don't have to worry if you are going to have a baby, when I think about it I know I would be proud of him or her. It doesn't seem possible that such a thing could happen to you, but I suppose we would soon get used to it. There is one thrill we haven't had yet dear, & that is feeling George slip inside you, but it's taking a big chance unless we didn't mind taking the chance of having a baby. I hope you understand Dear, & don't think I am rather crude. Don't take me wrong & think that I really want a baby now, & let me slip inside you when I get home, I don't want that to happen until you'r sure you want it to. I asked you in one of my letters what you thought about the subject, but you didn't tell me, but you can when I'm close to you next.

It's been pretty cold here the last few days, but it is nicer than the sloppy weather we had at first.

I got a film for my camera to-night, so I will try and take some pictures to-morrow.

Our exams start in the morning, but I don't feel like studying to-night, I guess it's the thought of leaving here soon that's making me feel happy & take a little less interest in things.

Well, Dear, look after yourself and prepare yourself for a hard night; it may be hard but it will be heavenly. We're not going out of each other's sight all the time I'm home if I can help it. We're going to make the best of every minute.

I'll write again to-morrow night, but you may not get it until after I get there.

So-long for now my most wonderful, beautiful & adorable wife & Sweetheart.

Your ever loving and worshiping husband.

XXXXXX   Don.

P.S. Where do you get the "Sergeant Major' stuff?

Mon, Feb. 3, 1941.

My Darling Wife:

Believe it not Darling, here I am in Westminster Hospital with the "measles". Cpl. Plumridge & I came in together. He is in my platoon you know, I don't know how no 9 is going to get along. We will be here for seven days anyway, so I guess there won't be much use you coming up this week-end. You couldn't come to see me because I am isolated.

I don't feel sick. I just finished a pretty goods dinner. We saw Capt. Foex at 8 a.m., & didn't get up here until 10 a.m. Then we saw another doctor at the main office & he said we had German Measles. So I guess we have "German Measles". We realy look cute.

Well, they had to put up another bed, getting kind of crowded. I guess we don't even have to stay in bed.

It sure is a swell day out here. The sun is just pouring in through the windows. I hope you don't have the measles too. Though you don't easily catch cold or sickness do you?

§ Ducky §

Did the fellows laugh at me this morning. They called it a "baby disease". The R.S.M. offered me .25 cents to let him wear my underwear so that he could be in the hospital too.

Well I guess I hadn't better write much more. They say it isn't good for the eyes to use them to much when you have the measles.

So-long for now my Darling. Please don't worry about me, I am fine. Don't forget I love you Sweetheart. Answer me soon, yours as ever.

Your loving husband Don.

I.P Bk's
London, Ont.

Dear Phyl:

I just happened to remember I promised to write to you. I haven't been home yet & I doubt if I will, but I may.

If you can, will you bring my swimming trunks & my green pants when you come. If you have no way of carrying them they aren't absolutely necessary, so you suit yourself

I guess I won't have a holiday Friday or Sunday & I don't know which guard I will be going on & when.

I can't think of much to say Dear, only don't stay away too long. I guess I miss you more than I thought I would.

Have a good time Darling, & I will give you another good time when you get home, I betcha.

That's about all Sweetheart. I hope to hear from you soon before you come home.

Lots of love & kisses.

XXXXXX   Don.

Michael W Dymond

Somewhere near Woodstock
30 July 41

Dear Phyl:

Well Darling, everything is going fine. We marched to Ingersol yesterday & slept in the arena. It rained like the dickens last night, or we would have slept in the open. We got soaked yesterday afternoon but we dried out pretty well.

To-day, no.9 platoon is riding because we are the rear guard & we leap-frog from sections of our truck.

The boys are standing up well. We marched about twenty miles yesterday & only about six are riding to-day.

I hope you can read this, I'm writing it on the ground. We are due in Hamilton Saturday noon & we are supposed to leave on the train Monday night.

You can write to me this week if you want to. Just address it to A Coy, Kent Regt., enroute from London to Hamilton.

I can't think of much else to say now Ducky. I'll mail this as soon as possible. We don't pass many mail boxes.

It's taken me four or five hours to write this & now it's nearly dark. We are in a school yard.

So-long for now Dear, I love you Darling as ever.

X
                                                    Don.

⚘ Ducky ⚘

To My Darling Wife:

Well Dear, what does it feel like to be an aunt "Auntie Phyllis", sounds swell. Harry got his telegram to-day, & he is probably home by now. I hope they are both doing fine.

Now about you & I Darling. How are you anyway? I'm fine. We marched through Hamilton to-day to Standard Barracks where we will be staying until sometime Monday. At least we have pollyasses to sleep on, & I hope to get a good nights sleep to-night & to-morrow night. The good old earth is all right when you get used to it. We were rained out twice, the second time we slept in a barn on hay & straw which wasn't too bad, but to-night we sleep in luxury. I wish it were at home beside my dear wife, but I guess I will have to put my arms around my kit-bag & close my eyes & imagine what I would be doing if it were realy you there.

Take a tip from me Darling & and find something to keep you busy all the time, it keeps you from thinking & making yourself unhappy. In few months you will have something to occupy your mind with & help take my place.

Darling, if you want to write to me so that I won't have to wait to long for a letter from you, I think if you address the letter to the Kent Regt., enroute to East Coast it will get me somewhere. I sure would like to hear from you.

I had a shower and & a swim here at the Y.M.C.A. this afternoon, & I sure feel better after that. I had supper here &

then went to a show & came back again to write to you & mum & dad.

I won't keep mentioning it to you Dear, but I want to hear an answer to your promise to me before I left. I know you don't like to be reminded about those things, but I want you to be well & happy & then so will I, & it will make things a lot easier for me as well as you.

That's about all for now Ducky, good night & God bless you & see you in the morning,

Your ever loving husband

X   Don.

Halifax N.S.
Monday, 1 Sept. 41
& tomorrow is the "2nd"!

To My Darling Wife:

Of a year, & not one day regretted. If a couple spent a better all around first year than we did, show me to them. We did everything on our own hook, started a home; with a family on the way & above all, loved the whole year out. The longer we are married, the more I love you, & realize that a wife is loved by a husband more than anything else in the world. Everybody else is in the background. I can't explain the feeling I have, knowing that though I am so far away from you, you carry within you a part of me. There is a part of both of us in there Darling that will soon be born a baby for both of us to love and adore. I guess that feeling I can't explain is realy love for you. Believe me Darling, everything I say is sincere.

I'm lying on my back in my pollyass in my tent, with the rain pouring down. Some kind of card game is in process on one side of the tent.

This afternoon I read a cowboy story & slept for a couple of hours. I don't think I told you the Duke of Kent will be here Thursday. I will tell you all about it later.

There is a possibility that we will be C.B. until Saturday, but I hope not.

There isn't much to do around here, so I shouldn't spend very much money. Yesterday I got the highest pay for quite a while. $18.20. I spent more money on cigarettes than anything else. I figure about .25 cents a day, approximately $7.50 per month. So I spent about ¼ of my pay on smokes. The rest on pop, the occasional beer, chocolate bars, I've been to one show, realy two shows, but I only got about a half hour of the second one and I got called back to barracks.

I think I will sign off for a while Dear. I can't mail this until the morning, so I may think of something else to say before then.

It is now 4 oclock Tuesday afternoon. We moved out of our tents last night & into a good hut, so we are all pleased & much happier. We did a fairly good days work to-day which is something to help along.

I received your card this afternoon, I was pleased but just a little unhappy because I hadn't been able to send you anything. If I can get down town before the store close I will send you something to remember me by, but I am still C.B. which is my only excuse.

I slept in the same bed above Cyril last night.

Well Darling so-long for now & be good to yourself, I'm good to myself – ha, ha!

Until tomorrow Ducky, your ever adoring husband,

X   Don.

Halifax, N.S.
Mon., Sept. 29

My Darling Phyl:

How are you to-day Sweetheart? I'm fine. No complaints at all.

There's some barn-dance music on the radio. A piano and fiddle, & all the fellows beating time on everything & making a hell of a noise in general.

No mail yesterday or to-day from you. I will probably get 2 or 3 to-morrow. It often happens that way.

I want to write a nice letter to you Darling, but I can't think of anything to say. I will try and write whatever comes into my mind, just for something to say, so it may be rather uninteresting.

I'll be going out to make my rounds later on this evening as usual, I go out 3 times a day regularly. I drive quite a bit too, so I am keeping in practice, which is more than I expected to do when I left home.

Tomorrow is pay day, & thank goodness for that. I'm broke & so is everyone else. And everyone is out of tobacco. Every man I meet says, "Whatcha smoking' Sarge." Some how or other I always seem to have a cigarette, & I haven't rolled any since before I left London.

Have you heard from mammy lately or been to see her again? And how are you making out with Mrs. McVeigh. I guess you wouldn't notice her fat tummy because she is fat anyway, or does that make any difference?

I see by the paper that Jim Spearman is in Valcartier, & doing quite well in the hurdles.

Are the trainers moving out of no. 12 B.T.C or is that just another rumour?

I think the Colonel will be back sometime this week, so there'll be some changes made. Joe Lewis is fighting his last fight to-night before he joins the army; 11;15 here, so I am going to try and listen to it.

There are deer up in this neck of the woods. O'Shea killed a copper snake & we found a lizard blowing bubbles so Cpl. Turner killed that too. We were even told there are bear around here too. Lots of sea-gulls and fish, of course.

I think I will quit writing for a while & maybe later I will think of something else to say; it's 6:40 p.m. now.

MON – 9:30 p.m.

Well Darling, I didn't get back to this letter last night. I went to sleep, & was awakened by the siren heralding an imaginary air-raid.

We came in from the coast to-day, so I hope now to be able to write to you more regularly.

We were paid to-day also, so I am that much more happy. My pockets, they jingle, oh boy! I hope I don't spend it all in one place.

I received a letter from you & your mum this evening & also a paper from Dad.

So Gert has a baby boy, well, good for her. She has succeeded permanently this time I hope.

You probably did see Sgt. Elliott, because I'm pretty sure he is in a course down that way somewhere.

So, you are starting on your bottom drawer are you. Maybe I could help you out in my spare time by crocheting some socks or maybe embroidering some diapers.

You go ahead & eat all you can Darling. But don't get too fat so I won't recognize you when next I see you. And when we do meet again, don't faint or just look at me with your mouth open, you run up to me & kiss me, because I know that is what I am going to do to you.

Don't worry Dear, if I come home sooner or later I will get real close to you, you wait & see.

I bought myself some shaving cream and tooth paste, and to-morrow I am going to try and go down town & buy myself some underwear shorts.

Happened to be a movie here to-night at 10 o'clock, but it's twenty mins past ten now, & no pictures!

Gosh Darling, I hope I get this letter finished. It's 1 p.m. Wed. now. I saw that picture last night but had to wait until about 11:30 because they had trouble with the machine. However, the picture was very funny & I enjoyed it, even though it was 1;15 before I got to bed. So I feel a bit tired to-day.

I bought myself $3.00 worth of cigarettes just now, & I hope they will last me until next pay-day.

I must write to Mum and Dad to-day, so I will say so-long for now.

Be good Ducky. I'm still hoping to see you not so very long from now. But I'm not building my hopes up, so I won't be disappointed. You do the same.

That's all Darling, from your ever loving hubby,

X   Don.

Citadel, Halifax, N.S.
Nov.2, 1941.

Hello Darling:

Well, I arrived here safely & the trip back was much faster than the one down but it actually took longer. When I arrived here I was surprised to find A Coy. was out on the coast. The Sgts. Mess had a party that night and Sgts. Kitchen and Smith where coming in to it so I waited & went back with them & arrived there soon after two in the morning. The Sgts invited the Women's Auxiliary Corps to the party & they came in uniform & the officers loaned us their mess. The party was a success but I didn't particularly enjoy it. I was too damned tired. I've realy been catching up on my sleep. I went to bed at 10:30 last night & didn't get up until 7:30 this morning and slept for a couple of hours this afternoon. Haven't done much to speak of all day.

Well Darling, how have you been feeling, I hope you haven't been bothered with that headache anymore.

My money has been working our better than I figured. I get about 33 dollars a month, I missed last pay & this time I only got about 2.50, so I don't owe the pay-master anything. I payed Ernie $10, so I only owe about 15 now, & it won't take me too long to pay that.

How is Dad coming along? I haven't heard anything since I got back.

Went to church service this morning like a good boy. It only lasted about 20 mins, shortest one I've ever attended.

Things are as ever here. Though it looks as if we are going to move pretty soon.

I worked most of yesterday making out tests for the men on gas. Looks as if I'm going to be pretty busy with that from now on.

On the way down on the train, another soldier from no 12 who was on his way to Sussex N.B, & I ran into a fellow on the train who had lots of money & a quart of whiskey, another fellow who also had a quart joined us & we had a good time in the smoker of the sleeper, singing, & talking about things in general. The fellow with all the money, he was a chemical engineer, bought us our supper Wednesday, $1.50 steaks. His bill was $6.30, & was that steak good. I couldn't eat any dessert.

There ain't much more to say Ducky. I think I'll be with you again before long, & then I hope it will be you & I together as man & wife instead of the way it was the last three weeks I was home. I know you didn't enjoy them Darling, & I'm sorry, but I guess it just couldn't be any other way. So you can look forward to some lovin' & happiness the next time I see you.

Cheer up Darling & look after that little tummy.

All my love as ever your hubby.

X   Don.

❦ Ducky ❦

M.P.O. 203 Niagara Camp,
Niagara-on-the-Lake,
Ontario.
Wed. 3 Dec. 1941

Hello Darling:

I guess you know by now. But believe it or not, I'm at the above address. Arrived here at 8.30 standard time, 9.30 this time, daylight saving time.

We left dear old Halifax Monday at 6 p.m. We sure were sorry to leave. Weren't we Dear?

As to when I will be home, I don't know. But it won't be long. I probably won't have time to let you know when I'm coming home, I'll just pop in when I get there.

Well, we are at least in an army camp & not in any make-shift barracks.

Right now we won't be doing guard duty. The way I understand it. We stay in this camp for a month & just do training. Next month we go to another camp in this district & do guard duty & then the following month to another camp for more guard duty then back to this camp again, & so on around again.

We hope to at least have more leave here.

Not a particularly interesting trip down here. I lost two men on the way down. We sent them out at a stop in Quebec to buy cigarettes and chocolate bars & the train left before they got back. I think they will show up tomorrow morning. I hope.

While I think of it Darling, I will write my correct address.

A49506
Sgt. Dymond D.W.
Kent Regt. (A),
M.P.O. 203
Niagara Camp
Ontario.

I haven't been out of camp yet, so I can't tell you anything about the scenery around here.

I didn't tell you in so many words I was leaving Halifax to come here, because that would be giving away a military secret. Though a lot of the men wrote home about it, so I'm sure you heard about it. Anyway, I'm here, which is the most important point.

It doesn't seem possible we are in good old Ontario again, it sure sounds good to us. I expected it to be cold here, but it isn't a bit.

I'm nearly broke Duck. I don't think I have enough to get home unless I hitch-hike. But money or no money, I'll get home. It may possibly be this week-end, but I'm not sure.

Anyway, when I do get home look out Darling. Because I am close to home now & I'll be getting hotter than ever because I know I'm so much closer to you, & only a few hours will bring me right to you. So beware!!!!!!!

Well Sweetheart, the main thing I wanted to tell you was: I'm here. So I will say so-long for to-day. God bless you Darling & I will be seeing you soon.

Forever, your loving husband.

X   Don

✦ Ducky ✦

Greetings Pal:

Well, another day has nearly all passed into history. Not a very eventful day. Just a normal one in a soldier's life. Went out to the rifle ranges this morning & damn near froze. It's been snowing since about ten this morning.

When I was coming in for dinner at noon the Sgt. Mjr. told me I was acting Sgt. Mjr. for the next five days while he is on his Xmas leave., & that's all he said. So here I am a Sgt. Mjr.

Didn't do much this afternoon. Went over to our indoor rifle range. Gord Chatterton was there & he said I could do some firing, so I spent about an hour and a half there.

We go out again to the outdoor ranges to-morrow (Sunday); the better the day, the better the deed. Yea?

I went to the show last night with Jerry, & enjoyed it. A double feature, "The Mummy's Hand", a bit spooky & not too bad; and: "Reaching For The Sun" which was very good, I haven't laughed as much for a long time.

If it keeps on snowing like it has done to-day, we will need snow shoes to walk with. Though it doesn't seem so cold as it was during the day. It's nearly 7.30 p.m. now.

I'm not certain, but I have an idea I may be home on 22 Dec., but I'll have to be back again on the 25th.

Cyril has gone away on a course in Quebec with Sgt's Kitchen, Bliech & Laurrie, but I believe they are home on Xmas leave now. Lucky beggars.

Well Sweetheart, there ain't no news. I haven't written very much but I'll try and write every day. I hope your cold is all better Darling. Be a good girl & look after yourself for me because it won't be so very long now, will it?

That's all for to-night Darling. Good night & God bless you. See you soon I hope.

All my love, your Sweetheart.

X   Don.

M.P.O. 203 Niagara Camp, Ont.
1.15 a.m. 31 Dec 1941.

Mornin' Darling!

There ain't much left of this old year & by the time you get this letter we will be well into 1942. I'll bet I forget to put 1942 on my letters for a long time.

Well, I've made my rounds this morning. My officer, Mr. Pineo, is going into Battalion Headquarters to-day until Friday, so I'm in charge again. Another man was just sent out to me so I am all set.

12.30 p.m. Finished my dinner so I think pretty soon I'll lie down and catch forty-winks. I'll have to be on nights now that my officer is leaving.

I wonder if you are getting my letters regularly. I seem to think that our mail service isn't very well looked after. But I am writing quite regularly.

Well kiddo, I'm stuck for news right now, so I think I will sleep on it & maybe even have a dream & tell you about it. O.K.?

70

Time has elapsed & it is 10 p.m. I got my snooze in this afternoon anyway.

I have a slight touch of indigestion. I had a half an onion for supper, it was a bit red inside & boy was it hot. Learn one day won't I?

I came awfull close to catching it this afternoon. When the ration truck came this afternoon I asked them to get me some water, so the driver told me I could take the truck & get it myself, so for the change I did & I took Pte. Sherwood with me. We went to a gas station on the outskirts of Niagara. While we were there along came Sherwood's sister-in-law on her way home with an armload of groceries. She lives about ½ miles the other side of our post from where we were then, so he yells at her & says we would take her home. So she comes over and dumps her groceries in on the seat. I should have refused to take her but I didn't have the nerve. So off we went & I was just rounding the curve near the post when I saw a station wagon stopped at the entrance & 3 officers walking down the steps to the huts. I stopped dead and let the lady out & drove on, quite expecting to be brought up about it, but for some unknown reason I couldn't have been seen. So I guess I got away with it. Lucky beggar!

Quite a night for New Year's Eve. Not very cold, snow on the ground & a white hazy mist over everything. Another 50 minutes and it will be 1942.

Well my Sweetheart, the whistles & the horns are blowing, it's twelve o'clock & we are all happy. The guard is being changed & they are wishing me a happy new year through the window. It's all over now & we are about two minutes into 1942. I wonder what is in store for you and I this year Darling. A very important thing we know for sure Ducky, and that is our family. If nothing else happens, what better could happen.

Everyone seems to have the idea the Brigadier or some of his staff are going to be around to-night, so we had better be on our toes.

Everyone seems to be on the phone wishing everyone else a happy new year. Hugh is on the line now talking to Joe. Just had a conversation with Hughie, poor Hughie. He doesn't get a pass this time. That's what he gets for missing his station, but he doesn't lose his stripes. Tranter lost his stripes and I believe Harry lost 20 days pay, but don't say anything.

A very thoughtful person in his car just gave the sentry on the bridge a couple of bundles of magazines for us. The people are a lot different here than they were in "Halifax". I wish this damn phone would stop ringing, it's a damn nuisance. And those damn train whistles! Chug-chug-chug! Clackety-clack, Clackety-clack! Whooo-ooo-ooo! Ting-a-ling-a-ling! No 10 post, Sgt Dymond speaking. Yes Sir! Blow it out your ass sir! Dear Mother – having a lovely time, wish you were here. The bullets they whistle, the cannons they roar. Bum-titty-bum-titty, bum-bum-bum.

There is not to reason why, There is just to do & die. Give us the tools and we will do the job! I've got a tool & I'm just the guy that can do the job. How about it Darling, are you in the mood? I am!

4.20 a.m. – Well Dear, it seems as though there is a German prisoner on the loose around here somewhere. We have to stop all cars crossing the bridge & make the people get out. Some fun eh kid?

5.30 a.m.- Still no prisoner. I've had a lot of fun making people get out of their cars. Nearly all have been out celebrating, though

None of them were realy drunk, just about three sheets in the wind. I guess they wonder what it is all about.

At least it has livened things up a bit, a change from doing nothing anyway.

Not many cars go by here at night, about one every ten or fifteen minutes, & that's quite a few because it is New Years.

Just got one gentleman without a registration card, he was tight.

Well my Sweetheart, I think I'll close now & get someone to mail this.

So-long & God bless you Darling. You know I love you.

As ever, your loving husband,

X   Don.

Many of his letters, perhaps written in haste, were difficult to read. As much as the writer would have loved to include all letters, verbatim, that would have been most difficult to do.

Nowhere in any of dad's letters did he reveal any weakness; no fear, and as said in many, he had no complaints. He would never appear weak in mom's eyes. He needed to be strong for her, as it was he that left. At times, however, a vestige of desperation would appear between the lines; a weariness and frustration with a war that was seen at the outset as being simple; home in six months sort of thing, but turned out to be quite different. War is never simple.

MORE ABOUT DONALD
AND PHYLLIS

Donald W Dymond, Circa 1940

Phyllis E Jackson, Circa 1940

Phyllis' upbringing was rather ordinary. She was born and raised in Chatham, Ontario, Canada. Phyllis' parents emigrated separately from England in the early nineteen-hundreds, arriving in Canada at different times. In search of work and hope, they found each other. Rose, her Mother, cleaned houses, took in boarders during the war and sat with children for a number of prominent families in the community. Billy, her father, labored for the City's works department.

Rose, strong willed, kept house and family in order, which meant for Phyllis and her sister, Shirley, a restricted and rather directed life. Shirley rebelled, did what she wanted and Phyllis towed the line afraid to even open her mouth. But they survived.

Donald arrived from England in nineteen twenty-eight with mother Dorothy, father Robert and a younger sister Vera Kate, who, sadly, passed on at the age of seven of a childhood disease.

Donald was loved and supported by his family. He attended school in Chatham; worked for the Eaton Company and later worked as a printer's assistant, type-setter at the Mercury Press. Eventually, duty called him to serve.

LETTERS OF 1942

M.P.O. 203, Niagara Camp, Ont.
6 Jan. 42 – 1 p.m.

Greetings My Love:

Ah! what a wonderful day. Bright & clear, & certainly chilly. It was damn cold this morning. One thermometer read 15° below zero. It's warmed up a bit since then.

Now about the place where I am now. It's realy a beautiful site. Up on top of a very high hill. We can see for miles around. St. Catherines is just below us, so it seems anyway, & they say we can see Grimsby & even Toronto on a clear day.

It's nearly four o'clock now & I've made my rounds. I guess it took me about two hours. It's a devil of a long way. I have to do that twice a day. In one place I have to go down and climb up nearly 400 steps. I did it once allready today, and it sure is a hard grind.

Whoops Dearie: The Brigade Major just popped in, & he just went in to one of the other huts. I suppose he will be back again. Doesn't seem to be a bad sort of fellow.

That old wind has started to blow again & it's snowing too. Promises to be a real wintry night. At least we have a good stove here.

While I think of it Darling, would it be too much trouble for you to send me the words of "To-night We Love.?"

Mr. Pineo also has a nice little radio here.

The rations just came so we eat for a while.

Just made myself a lamp shade for my extention, out of a writing paper box.

Realy a blizzard blowing now Darling. The snow even blows in through the cracks.

Must be nearly supper time, guess I'll go and see. See ya' later!

-later- I feel better now. I had a good supper. But the weather doesn't sound any better. Blowing & snowing worse than ever. Going to be hard to keep this place warm to-night I betcha.

If my writing is a bit crooked, it's because I can't see the lines very well through the paper. At least you won't be seeing the patern on your wall through this paper when you read my letter.

I wish the snow would stop blowing in on me. My table is wet now. I hope I don't wake up covered with snow in the morning.

I almost forgot. Last night when we got back, the R.S.M. told Ernie and I we had to sleep in another room because they had found a bed-bug in one of the Sgt's beds.

I left my other uniform & some of my equipment in the barracks to be fumigated. I hope they send my uniform out to me soon, because I don't want to wear my good uniform out here all the time.

I think I had better go out & tie this shack down before it blows away.

I asked the C.Q. to get me a dollars worth of tobacco & papers, so I think that will last me until pay-day. I still will have a buck left.

Wed-7- 8:10 a.m.

I'll write until I get too cold & then I'll quit. Boy, is it ever cold. The stove on the other side of this hut is red hot, but it must be freezing here. I have two sweaters on & a blanket around me.

It took me almost three hours steady going to do my rounds last night, so I thought that was enough exercise to put me to sleep for the whole night, but it was so cold I don't know how many times I woke up.

Well Darling, it's too uncomfortable sitting here so I am going to sign off. I'll probably start another letter tonight.

So-long now Sweetheart, & God bless you. And you stay in where it's warm, won't you?

All my love for ever,

X   Don

M.P.O. 203 Niagara Cam, Ont.,
7 Jan 42. 5 p.m.

Dear Loved one:

Just to be different Darling I'll say "I love you" to begin with. That is the most important thing so shouldn't it come first?

I haven't seen any mail at all to-day. The C.Q. was here but I don't think he brought any. Maybe someone else will bring some, & maybe there will be one from you, I hope.

Still pretty damn cold here. 4 below zero so the school teacher told me this morning. There is a school down here, & of course all schools must have teachers. The school is about a twenty minute walk from here. I waved to some kids in the window & when I passed the gate, about four of them came tearing out & asked me if I wanted to come in and warm myself. I accepted their invitation & forthwith proceeded into the class room. There I spent a little while warming myself, talking to the teacher & listening to the kids. The class is about 30 strong but only about 6 showed up to-day, because of the weather, so they were having a bit of a holiday. And don't think I didn't appreciate that nice fire. I-we all- damn near froze last night. I didn't even get a good sleep, & it's not a lot better to-day. I guess we'll pull through O.K., don't you?

I wish the boss would get in so I can eat. Maybe he stopped at the school to get warmed up. tsk.tsk. These soldiers!!!?

Well Kiddo, I've started to roll-my-own again. Smitty brought me my tobacco this afternoon –

-

Thurs 8 – 3p.m.-

At last it is nearly comfortably warm in here. My God, it has been cold. 5 below this morning. I've been warmer making my rounds than beside the fire.

I was just wondering Ducky, if it would be a good idea if I didn't come home on my next leave, & save the five dollars & come home when you will realy want me home. But it you want me to come home on my next leave, I will. You tell me what you think. I'll be home anyway when you want me, no matter how often I come home.

Quite a bit of snow around here Darling. Some places where I have to go it's up to me knees in drifts.

As usual Sweetheart, there isn't much to talk about. It realy is a swell day. It's real cold but the sun is shining.

I only woke up twice last night. I had an extra blanket and there wasn't much wind.

❦ Ducky ❧

Once again I have started to listen to the happy-gang again.

I should have a letter from you to-day. If there isn't I'll be a bad boy when I come home, If!?

The boss has just gone out to make his rounds. I guess we each spend about six hours every day making rounds. That's one reason why it isn't as monotonous as it was on the other post. We aren't couped up behind wires & locked gates as we were. I have to go about a half-mile down the road to one of our posts, so I do get out.

Gee, Ducky, it doesn't seem possible that very soon I will be a father. Only a while ago I was going to school & running errands after four. It's surprising how time flies & things happen. I just can't seem to realize that I am not a boy any longer. I still can't realize I'm 22 years old. Oh well, what does age or what happens matter as long as we are happy.-

I love my wife,
She's the girl of my dreams.
As I sit here and think,
To me it seems,
That just yesterday
We walked arm in arm
'Neath the stars & the moon,
And we dreamed of these charms:
That some day soon
We would be man & wife;
And that I would spend
All the rest of my life
Making you happy
And giving you things

81

That wives should expect.
Without saying it, brings
From my heart, as we know
Those three little words,
Just, "I Love You."

I started this letter yesterday, Ducky, & now it's gone five o'clock to-day, & I haven't mailed it yet. I must give it to someone to-night so that you won't be too long not hearing from me.

Take care of yourself for me Darling, & God bless you & ours. So-long from your ever loving hubby,

X   Don

M.P.O. 203 Niagara Camp, Ont.,
9 Jan. 42. – 3:45 p.m.

Lo Pal:

What'cha' hear from the mob?

The weather here ain't no better. Not quite so cold but blowing hard, & it snowed quite a lot again last night. But, we seem to have the hut warmed up at last.

I imagine maybe I'll have a letter from you this afternoon, I hope!

I haven't shaved to-day yet. I'm getting to be quite a soldier aren't I?

Mr. Crummer had a hard time getting through with his truck to-day. Had to detour because of snow drifts. I hope

𝕾 Ducky 𝕰

Smitty gets through with the ration truck. At least we have lots of coal to last us more than a day.

For some reason or other Darling, I can't seem to write nicely on this paper. I'm trying hard but it doesn't seem to work.

The water lines all froze up at the barracks, so I don't know when I'll get my laundry done. I'll be needing clean clothes pretty soon.

Would you like me to wax poetical again? Maybe something silly this time. At least it will fill up the paper:

TITLE: "Oh! What The Hell."

Up here where I am the wind blows cold,
It blows snow through the cracks & between the fold
Of my blanket, and tickles
My spinal column,
And I shiver and shake from top to bottom.

The Pioneer Platoon is supposed to repair
What's broken down and busted from wear and tear.
I think those buggars don't come around
'Cause they don't know their ass from a hole in the ground.

There's nothing to do but sit here and shiver,
And look out the window on what was a river.
But it's dead, and I'm dead, and I don't know why,
So I'll sit here and listen to the snails wiz by.

Twice in twenty-four hours, by night and by day,
From post to post in a soldierly way

I walk in snow that's up to my knees,
It's a wonder my nose and my___don't freeze.

As long as the coal and rations come through
We at least keep warm and we always have stew,
So, if the boys pound their beats and do their job well,
We shall all be happy. Oh, what the hell!

Still no mail from you Sweetheart. I suppose there is realy nothing for you to say. It was only four days ago that I was home with you and I'll be able to come home again in six days. So why should I complain.

It's six o'clock already. This afternoon has sure gone fast.

I sowed my Canada badges on my great coat and good uniform this afternoon, but I don't think I did a very good job on them.

There's work to be did now Ducky. So I must sign off.

So-long Sweetheart, take care of yourself & God bless you. Always your loving hubby, all my love.

X   Don

M.P.O. 203 Niagara Camp, Ont.
10 Jan./42.

Hi Ya Baby:

Night is drawing nigh, & the mercury is dropping again. Sounds as if the wind is rising again. Promising to be a delightful evening. Between the weather and the snow on the ground, it is starting to get monotonous doing the rounds. Care to know where I go.

I start out on the other side of the canal and walk down the dyke for nearly mile. Then I go out through a gate & down the road about ½ mile, turn off down the hill on another road, across a bridge, through a fence, through a field beside a river, over a small damn & on to the post about 200 yds further. Then I turn around and go back, past where I started, down a 250 foot hill and 170 steps, around a power house to the other post & then back here again. I do that in the morning, starting about 8. Generally takes me nearly three hours each time. Quite a little jaunt. But that little walk makes it just that much less monotonous. I realy don't mind it here at all.

By the way; guess what! I got a letter from you to-day. My, my.

So it's cold there too is it? It's been 3 & 5 below zero here every night, & damn close to it during the day.

Yes, Sweetheart, between myself & the rest of the gang we ate the food I had on the train.

You had some funny pains did you my Darling? So I guess maybe it won't be long. I guess you feel, the sooner the better, don't you Darling. I'm thinking about you & _it_ all the time Darling.

I can sit by the stove all right Darling, but sometimes you bake on one side & freeze on the other. We have had no trouble with the lights here.

Thanks for the words of my song Darling.

So Shirley is sick, is she? Ain't that too bad. That much more work for you. But you take it easy.

I'm getting a bit chilly here, so I think I will go over by the fire. See you later Ducky.

Michael W Dymond

Sun.- 12:45 p.m.

Here I am again Sweetheart. What a hell of a day. It isn't so very cold. But it's blowing great guns, and is the snow ever drifting. I was walking along the side of the road in a drift this morning and I went down the full length of my legs.

I'll bet the trucks have a hard time getting through. One thing good: I never get cold when I am out. As a matter of fact, I am always sweating when I get back from my rounds. The only place I get cold is here in the hut, & then it isn't bad.

I pressed my winter cap yesterday afternoon. I think I will wear it home the next time. It is much warmer, & it doesn't look too bad now that it is pressed.

You can figure out a title for this one Darling.

Very soon you'll be a mother,
And of course I'll be a Daddy too.
I wonder what it's like to be parents,
I'll bet I won't know what to do.

I'll come and see you when they let me,
I won't know whether to grin or not.
I'll probably stand there in the door-way
And look like a thinker without a thought.

Then I'll come in a kneel beside you
And smile and look into your eyes,
And with all my heart I'll say, "I love you:"
More than maybe you realize.

86

§ Ducky ?

They won't let me stay very long the first time,
The nurse will come in and I'll hear her say,
"You five minutes is up, you must be leaving,
She mustn't have too much excitement to-day."

So I'll get up slowly & kiss you good-bye,
At the door I'll look 'round and I'll see you smile,
And I'll give you one of my special winks
And say, "So-long Ducky, I'll be back in a while."

Gee, Darling, the sun is shining, but the wind she still blow.

Mr. Pineo just went out on his rounds. He hitched a ride on a snow plough, that should get him there if anything will.

Mr. Crummer should be along soon in his truck so I'll finish up now, so as to be sure he gets it to mail.

So-long now Darling, I hope those old pains haven't been bothering you. God bless you my Sweetheart, I love you so Darling.

All my love for ever,

X   Don

M.P.O.203 Niagara Camp, Ont.,
4:30 p.m. 12 Jan. 42.

Dear Girl of My Dreams Come True:

Just received your letter of Fri. & Sat. Sure was glad to get it.

I'm awful sorry to hear about Mum's legs, & it's a bit of a surprise to hear it's going to take that long for Dad to get better. Guess I had better write to them.

Yes Ducky I'll be off guard Thursday & it will probably be Thurs. before you get my (this) letter. It's Mon. to-day, if you haven't already guessed it.

Snookie's cutting teeth is he. Why can't they be born with their teeth, it would save a lot of sleepless hours.

I'm doing O.K. on my steps Ducky, though they are getting to be a bit of a nuisance. It took me a good six minutes to come up to-day.

There's that "Chatonoga Choo-Choo", again. Pardon me boy.

I didn't have the bugs. The idea, me lousy. Somebody else· had it. I'll have bugs pretty soon though. I sent my laundry in, but they have no water in barracks, the pipes are all frozen, so I'm getting a bit itchy. Itch-itch!

Ya likea my verse, ha? I'm musta read them when I'm comes home, ya? I betcha. Sucha talks, maybe you tinks I'm craze. New ???(just turn it around)

I think I'm a silly S---B- too. Gimme a shine. On track 29. A-choo-a choo!! Zip-zip!

Cold you say? Cold as a nun's cunt. And I imagine that's pretty cold. Imagine going all through life and never having your pussie warmed up for you. Why that's what it is for, isn't it darling? How do you think you would get along without ever having George inside you?

Just thinking about it Darling has made George all hot & hard. And it's not good weather he's standing up for. I wonder if I could write a verse about those things. I don't know what I would do if I couldn't put George inside you Ducky. I wouldn't want to put him anywhere else. He goes inside you so easily, he just fits right doesn't he. I can feel him there now. So nice & warm, & he slides in & out so easily. I love you so much down there Darling. That's why I love you there Sweetheart, & like to kiss you there. Just wait until after our baby is born, will we ever go to town. I'll keep kissing you then until you get so hot you slip. ---

---11.00 p.m. – had to leave you Darling, but I'm back again.

I got through my rounds earlier to-night. I just came from the kitchen, had some tea and toast.

One of my boys, - Bunda-, caught a muskrat to-night, skinned it & I guess they are going to eat it to-morrow.

It's not cold out to-night at all. I wouldn't be surprised if we had a thaw tomorrow.

Hugh says there is a fellow who leaves here at midnight & he will take our mail in for us, so I will finish this up to-night and mail it.

Nothing has happened around here. Nothing ever does anyway.

I'll be darned if I can think of anything else to say. I stay up until midnight because Mr. Pineo sleeps untill then. So I have nothing to do for an hour.

I guess I told you there is a new generating plant going in here. They are tearing down the hill-side now, & they do a lot of blasting too. One explosion shook the countryside. They are working day & night, seven days a week.

I left a pair of my shoes in barracks to be repaired & now Smitty says he can't find them, & I have walked so much these last few day, these shoes I have on are fast wearing out. –

Hugh & I were just outside trying to catch another muskrat, but no luck yet. We may get him yet.

Well darling, I must cut it short & be sure I catch the mail man. If I don't hear anything from you about coming home on Thursday, I guess I'll be there. Maybe I will have a letter from you to-morrow telling me which you want me to do, I hope so any way. So I'll be seein' ya sometime in the very near future.

So-long now darling, be good to yourself & may God bless you.

As ever in love with you,

X   Don

M.P.O. 203, Niagara Camp, Ont.

13 Jan, 1942

Hello Shrimp!

Boy, isn't it a wonderful day.

I no sooner get started on this letter than I am told dinner is ready. But I'm back again (12:15) & I had a good dinner.

Since I started this letter, only half an hour ago, the sky has clouded up. It was realy nice this morning. Nippy, but bright and cheery.

I only finished my last letter at midnight last night, so the Lord only knows what I am going to put in this one. No doubt, just a lot of nonsense.

3 p.m. I received a letter from you this afternoon. Your letters are what I look forward to most when I am out on these posts. At any time as far as that goes Darling.

✦ Ducky ✦

I'll bet Nora had a wild story to tell you about her New Years holiday.

I made up the verse myself Darling, I'm glad you like it. Maybe I could figure out some more some time.

I think I can get away when you want me Sweetheart. I haven't heard anything definite from you about coming home on Thurs, so I guess I'll be there. You haven't fallen down on your writing Darling. I have an idea how you must feel in your condition. I know you will write to me as often as you can. I know my wife loves me.

Yes Darling it is hard to believe, you having a baby; but as you say, from the looks of things it must be true.

Do you think maybe you won't be having dinner at home next Sunday. I guess you aren't quite sure are you. But we will see. If I don't hear anything different from you by Thursday, I will probably be home.

One of the boys just caught a rabbit. I guess it's dead and skinned now. We are quite a bunch of trappers and hunters here aren't we.

Well, Ducky, I will finish up now so that I can give it to Smitty.

See you soon, Darling, & keep up the good work & the chin for me. I love you Sweetheart as I always will. God bless you Darling, as ever yours.

Don

M.P.O. 203, Niagara Camp, Ont.
18 Jan. 42.

Zip-zip!

How's things kid.

We arrived in barracks O.K. last night. We had a wonderful trip.

This was funny. Three Cpls. & myself went back to the diner for a ham sandwich and coffee. I was hungry so I decided to cast care to the winds & blow my .50 tobacco money. Weren't we surprised when we were handed a bill for $2.40. Wasn't that outrageous, son-of-a-gun. My-oh-my. We couldn't get over it.

Well, here I am back at Queenston power plant again. I got wild again and busted my five spot for tobacco, so now I only have $4. I wonder how long that will last. I hope.

It has been very mild to-day. Though the weather doesn't matter to me. I am inside all the time anyway. All I have to do is go up and down the elevator and visit my two posts which are only the length of the generator building apart.

Just finished my supper, & I feel full.

My headache has gone & I feel O.K. Funny how I got that headache wasn't it. Guess I'll bring some canned Niagara air home with me the next time. Zip-zip!

I'm on duty now until mid-night. It's 6:35 p.m. now. Pretty soon I am going to lie down & have a snooze or I'll be tired before morning.

They are repairing one of the generators here. They are large things. Eight men working inside it didn't take up any room at all. If I can I'm going to watch them put it back together.

I have a picture that Art Davis took of me, hope it meets with your approval. I don't know who that guy is in the background. It looks like Charlie Dickie. It was taken just outside the door to the Sgt's quarters at Allenburg barracks.

-10 p.m. Here I am, back again. I just got back from Allenburg. I went in the truck and got some cigarettes, tobacco, chocolate bars, etc. so now I am the proprietor of a canteen. Zip. zip.

I've sold .50 worth of merchandise all ready. The only trouble is, there isn't any profit. Oh well, it will be something to do. -.60- I only have $10.40 worth left to sell now. I hope I keep my money straight. I remember once when I was treasurer of the A.Y.P.A. I got things all twisted up. Maybe I will profit by that mistake.

Anyway, I drove the truck 28 miles, into barracks & back. First time I have driven since I was in Halifax. And was it ever nice driving. It was raining a bit, & splash from other cars on the windshield and the windshield wipers wouldn't work. Some fun, just like flying blind.

-12:30 a.m. Monday.

Here I am again Darling. Sitting behind my counter watching the crowds go by. Should do a little bit if business now. The boys come up for their midnight soup, tea and bread.

I have an awful temptation to eat up the profits. But there ain't no profits. Guess I can hold out. I had one chocolate bar, but I payed myself for it. So I won't lose money that way will I? Or will I?

I haven't told you how I started this canteen, have I?

Well, the fellows are always wanting smokes or something when they are out on post, so I decided on a canteen. How did I finance it? One of my boys gave me $15.00 to save for him. So I said to myself, "I'm a bank, & all banks make use of the money they look after, so I'll do the same thing." So I used that money. I told the fellow who owned it about it & he said he didn't care. That's how I got my start. Not bad eh?

4:30 a.m. I'm getting a bit sleepy. Haven't slept since 6 yesterday morning. John McLagan has to get up now to start breakfast so I must go and awaken him. Gosh, he was awake when I got to his bed. He must have had a guilty conscience. Just one minute from the time I said I was going to awaken him & he is getting on with the breakfast.

It's still raining here. A very dirty night it has been. Such extremes of weather we do have.

It might be a good idea if I conjure up a bit of poetry, but I'm too tired.

There doesn't seem to be much more to talk about.

I've made my rounds & I met the Major going on his rounds on my way back.

I suppose I will have to open my canteen again at breakfast time, so I probably won't get to sleep untill late.

Looks like I'll have to use your $5. to get home with next time Sweetheart. I had another chocolate bar just now & I must buy a book of stamps so I can mail you this one.

They took too many men & too much equipment on one of the elevators yesterday morning & something went wrong & the damn thing dropped four or five floors & buried on the bottom, but not enough to cause any harm. I guess the boys held their breaths for a bit. Must have been a funny feeling.

My writing is pretty wrotten this time Darling. I guess because I am a bit sleepy, anyway it's a letter & a little longer than I expected it to be.

Well, I hope I hear from you today. If I don't, I won't be really disappointed.

Well my Darling, keep up the good work, & very soon you will be rewarded with the most wonderful thing that has ever happened to you. And we will both be so happy, won't we Sweetheart.

So-long for now my Darling Wife, & God bless you & be with you very closely for the next few days. Don't forget you have all my love to help you along. Always remember that Darling, it will help.

For ever your adoring husband,

X   Don

M.P.O. 203 Niagara Camp, Ont.
12:15 a.m. 20 Jan,/42

A Very Good-Morning Darling:

I am fine, how are you? The weather here isn't bad. How is it there?

Isn't that a hell of a way to begin a letter?

No letters from you yet. I get awfully impatient don't I? I don't give you a moments piece of mind. No doubt I will hear from you tomorrow. If I don't, I'll give you hell all over again. Of course, that doesn't mean anything does it? I don't think I really know how to give anybody hell.

I went into Allenburg again this afternoon, didn't I? How the devil would you know if I went to Allenburg? Wasn't that a silly thing to say?

Anyway, I went in to get some more stock for my canteen. My business is running smoothly. I hope it all adds up correctly in the end. I collected ten dollars more to invest in my blossoming enterprise, which makes twenty-five bucks in the business, besides a dollar or so of my own money that somehow or other slipped into the cash box, I'm not quite sure how much, but I'm afraid my five dollars is going to look a bit pale when the final day of reconing arrives. A chocolate bar here & a package of gum there soon starts a pocket book on the downward trend. Oh well, what's the use of living if you don't have those little enjoyments once in a while.

I finally got some sleep this morning, after twenty-five hours without any. If I get too tired to-night I'm darn well going to lie down and sleep.

I'm not sure whether we will be payed before our next leave or not. The general opinion is that we won't. Our next leave is due on the 27th, but don't bank too much on it.

In any case I'll be home when you want me. So from the general aspect of things I will need that five-spot you have saved. I don't really like the idea of taking it Darling, but I think it is better than borrowing, because I owe about $12 now. I want to get that payed up & then I can try again to save some money. Though saving money doesn't seem to one of my traits.

Business doesn't seem to be particularly booming to-night. Expect I shall sell more at breakfast time in the morning.

Guess what I would like right now. You don't know? Well, it's a real nice little fix. I guess it will be quite a while before the next one won't it Darling? But I don't mind a bit. You can always hold George can't you, & make him slip, & maybe I'll be able to hold you too; though someone else will be sucking your breasts. It's all going to be realy worth while missing a few little fixes for.

Won't it be wonderful when we will be able to get together again Darling, & I'll be able to lie on top of you like we used to, & both of us get real hot & just go wild. I'll be able to put George inside of you & put my hands on your bum & push him in real hard, all the way. And we'll roll over & over with him still inside you. I hope you are looking forward to it as much as I am. I hope that doesn't sound selfish to you Darling.

Well Sweetheart, I will finish this letter now so I can give it to the patrol officer to mail. He should be in pretty soon.

So until the next letter Darling I'll say so-long & God bless you, & look after junior.

For ever your hubby in love with you,

X   Don

M.P.O. 203, Niagara Camp, Ont.,
21 January 1942, 2:10 p.m.

Dear Phyl:

Hello Darling, how is my dear wife to-day. I'm out of writing paper so I have to resort to the good old Starvation Army stationery.

Guess what? We moved again this morning. I'm not quite as important this trip, if I should put it in that way. I have a post of my own, not two or three to look after as I have done before. I have ten men and a very nice hut to stay in. A real toilet and wash basin & and an electric hot water heater & lots of room. We are short of N.C.O.s, so I had to take this post. We are supposed to have some new N.C.O.s any time so I may not be here very long.

I am hardly a mile from the falls. I saw them this morning & they are pretty well all frozen up. We only passed them in the truck so I didn't get a real good look at them.

It's really a swell day Darling, a bit chilly but the sun is shining. I think I am going to like it here.

By the way, the Happy Gang are on. Their program is dedicated to the yankies, no doubt you heard them. It's good to hear them again. Once in a while I get snatches of them, but to-day I heard the whole program.

At the Queenston power plant one of the generators burned out & I watched them repair & partly replace it. They put the rotor – that's the part that turns – in last night with two cranes. The rotor weighed 313 tons, quite a large piece of machinery. It was very interesting.

I forgot to mention that I received your letter of last Monday. Having trouble with Shirley as usual are you? Oh well Darling, I guess there isn't much we can do about it. At least, it you take your mum's room you will be a little further away from her. It's damn nice of gram to give you her room. It will be a little more like a home of your own.

You mentioned about sending me the Star, thanks Darling, I will realy appreciate that. I always did like to follow up Tarzan & Buck Rogers etc. And there is nearly always a good novel in it.

♫ Ducky ♫

Just had a call from H.Q. & they are sending me out another man whom I need. And tomorrow they are sending out two N.C.O.s so I guess I will be leaving for Platoon H.Q. to-morrow. I think I'd rather stay here, I seem to like it.

Well, Darling, I'm glad to hear you still love me, as if I didn't know it all the time. And of course there is no doubt in your mind that "I love you". Like I've said so many times before you are more to me than anything else in this old world, more & more all the time. It seems that every time I come home I want to hold you close to me & kiss you more and more.

Well Sweetheart, I expect the officer around very soon so I will put a finish to me literary scrawl with the usual "so-long now, & God bless you."

For ever & ever your lover

X   Don

M.P.O. 203, Niagara Camp, Ont.,
1 a.m. 23 January, 1942.

Hello My Sweetheart:

Another day has begun Darling so I'll see if I can't think of something new to talk about.

I wonder if I can keep the lines straight instead of going up all the time. After a little practice I'll probably get along all right.

Just for a start I'll answer the letter I got from you to-day.

So you broke into your five too did you. Now I wonder how I will get home to see our infant and my wife. I'll get there you may be sure.

So McVeigh's a "pop" eh? I haven't seen him since Sunday. I have an idea he has gone away on a demonstration platoon of picked men from the brigade.

Glad you like my picture.

You had trouble with your stove did you? Well, I've had trouble with ours to-night. The wind seems to be in the wrong direction & the smoke keeps blowing out the top of the stove. I finaly got the smoke problem beat by leaving the back door open, now I've got to baby it along & make it burn. I think we got in a bad lot of coal, it stinks like hell.

That's okay by me if you go to St Joseph's Hospital Darling, I think I like it best too.

I didn't do a heck of a lot today. I went to bed about 7:30 this morning & got up soon after twelve noon. I helped Joh put up a rifle rack and beyond that I didn't do very much. I slept for a couple of hours this evening so I guess I will be able to keep awake until breakfast time, I hope.

I think I'll stop writing for a while & take a walk around & see if my sentries are on the job. – Back again, & everything seems pretty well under control. Not very cold out to-night.

Everyone but me seems to be a sleep in here. I have the radio on very quietly. My bed looks very inviting. I feel like lying on it with you Darling. I feel like a real passionate little fix right now. What ever am I going to do the next few week for my fixes, maybe I'll have to go out and buy some strange ones. They say a change is as good as a rest, but I doubt it Darling. You and I go together too perfectly.

Well Darling, cookie is getting breakfast so I'd better get things straightened around. So-long now my own dear wife & God bless you.

Your ever loving hubby,

Don

M.P.O. 203, Niagara Camp,
24 January, 1942.

Hello Gorgeous:

Here is me again at 12:45 a.m. Saturday morning. Listening to a story on the radio about the Incas of South America. There are some peculiar programmes in the early morning.

How is everything going Darling? I'm sure you are getting along fine. I guess you are pretty tired of carrying that weight around aren't you Ducky? It won't be for much longer Sweetheart & then you will have something else new to occupy your mind. I know you are going to love being a mother, & you're going to be a good one too. I've got all the confidence in the world in you Sweetheart. You don't know just how proud I am of you Darling.

Everything is going fine here Ducky. I was told the Colonel would be around to-night but it's one o'clock now & he hasn't shown up yet. He can come when he wants to, I'll be here all night.

I didn't have a letter from you to-day but no doubt I will to-morrow. I wrote to mum and dad last night.

Did I tell you that a lady across the street did our washing for us. They are Ukrainian. There are still some thoughtful people left in the world.

2:30 a.m. Just woke the next relief up & made some tea. Since I quit writing I moped the kitchen floor & scrubbed it too with a long handled scrub-brush. The Major and Patrol officer have been here but Tommy "Slug" - the Colonel – hasn't shown up yet.

Gosh, I feel tired. I sure would like to lie down and go to sleep. I've still got about four hours more to go. I'd better go out in the fresh air & blow the cobwebs out of my eyes.

There is a shower in the transformer station so I think I'll take a bath to-night. I've had one shower since I've been back & a change of clothes & I have clean clothes now to put on so I won't be so sweaty & dirty as I was at the last post.

I still can't seem to write straight. Maybe if I go down on the end of each line I will learn to stop going up. I'll make a regular caterpillar out of this by the time I get through. Maybe I can make a pretty design out of my letters by going up & down. Whenever – don't we have lots of fun. Whoops dearie, I'm going off my rocker again.

I'm getting silly now aren't I? Guess I had better wise up. But I've got to write & there isn't anything to write about so I'll just have to ramble along & fill up the paper. It didn't cost me anything anyway.

Oh damn, I'm so tired I can't even think of anything nonsensical to write so I guess I'll give it up as a bad job & see if I can't do better to-morrow night. So I'll be seeing you then Darling.

So-long now Darling & don't forget I'm thinking about you always. Please God bless you and keep you happy for me. One thing above everything else I want you to be well & happy. I love you Darling, oh; so very, very much.

All my love

X   Don

M.P.O. 203, Niagara Camp, Ont.,
24 January, 1942.

To My Lovely Wife:

Here is me, your husband, again Darling, who belongs to you, body & soul. I'm thinking about you all the time Sweetheart. Coming home to you so much more than I did in Halifax seems to make me want to be with you more & more. I miss you more than I ever did. I guess because you are going to have a baby makes me feel more that way.

It doesn't seem quite fair that you have to put up with all the trouble & suffering of having a baby & I don't have to do anything. But I suppose that is the way it is meant to be, but you know if there is anything I can do to help you along I will Darling. I'll do anything for my wife.

Sunday – 25 – 12:45 a.m. I had a list of work to do but I'm back again & listening to a program dedicated to the birthday of President Roosevelt. Edgar Bergen and Chuck McCarthy were just on. Something about the March of Dimes. Sounds as if it might be a good programme. Someone is singing "Ave Maria" – Deanna Durbin. Fibber McGee & Molly were on, Jimmie Cagney & many others. They are singing the American National Anthem now.

I wonder what the next programme will be.- The music of Shep Fields. Another station, they are playing our National Anthem, "God Save the King." I love that piece more every time I hear it. Three times they play it, the first time moderately more like an introduction, the second time very lightly like a hymn, & then as if all the famed bands in the world were massed & each man playing with his heart and soul, as if our armies were returning from battle, victorious & those who have been beaten & made to put up with unknown hardships & heart-aches are once more restored to what is rightfully theirs.

Another station Darling & a violin is playing & it makes me feel very quiet & a bit unhappy.

James Cagney & Maureen O'Sullivan were being married on the radio just now & they spoke their thoughts through the service. As they were standing there & the minister was repeating the service they both said they were very unhappy & now they didn't want to be married. They both were very much in love with each other, but there was a war on & like so many people, especially soldiers, that I have heard, at the last moment they thought that it wasn't right. But as the minister's thought said, at a time like this there should be more marriages & more children, we must think of the future. Civilization must go on after the war & it is up to us to prepare for it now.

Any couple that thinks for some reason or other that they shouldn't marry until the war is over, maybe because he will come back probably married for the rest of his life, or she or both of them may find someone else to love while they are separated – have no confidence in the future. They won't have children because they don't want to bring children into a world that no doubt will be a hell. That is so very selfish Darling.

We must have confidence in the future Darling. We must make up our minds & have no doubt at all that we are going to win. We don't know what the future has in store for us, & it doesn't have a very bright outlook. But no matter what is coming, we must face it & be prepared for it. After all Darling, what are we put on this earth for anyway. There is a reason for everything. In these next few years there are going to be drastic changes. Hard work, & unhappiness, we can look forward to it. We cannot exactly look into the future so we aren't sure what we are going to have to put up with. It is said that this war can bring only hardship. It seems only that we are here to put up with these things, so I guess that is the reason we are put here.

But that reason doesn't make me unhappy Darling. I am so absolutely sure in my mind that in the end we will obtained happiness, & it we work as our hearts tell us to, a happiness derived from knowing that we have done what we could to brighten the future for those that come after us, our children.

And Darling, for just you & I there is this very happy prospect. That you & I will be working together as two can only work together when their love for each other is complete and undying. And working with the thought that there is a goal to be obtained.

In a very short while we will have something to work for.

Keep these thoughts in mind Darling when you become a mother. Know in your heart & practice in your life that what I have said, not because I said it, because there is nothing else. And know that what I have said is from my heart & I firmly believe it to be so.

I'm a nice clean boy Darling because I had a bath to-night. There is a nice new shower room in the transformer station.

Well Sweetheart, I think I have written about enough for to-night so I'll save some ink for my next letter.

So-long now Phyllis & God bless you. I'll be seeing you soon. And I do love you so.

As ever your hubby,

Don

M.P.O. 203, Niagara Camp, Ont.,
1 a.m. 26 January 1942

Dear Phyl:

I'm running out of salutations, so this time it is a simple one but definitely to the point.

Here I sit & another day is off to a good start. Sherwood and Walker have just finished playing crib & they are off to bed, so very soon I'll be the only man to defend this fort, except of course for the sentries outside. But I kind of like the quietness of night. It gives me a chance to think & write to you, except if I'm tired.

Old Sherwood is spinning some of his yarns. He's pretty good and funny too. Wish I was as brainy as that old duck.

There is nothing on the radio so I have turned it off. I don't think this will be a very long letter Darling. I'll finish it pretty soon so I can give it to the patrol officer & have it mailed as soon as possible.

§ Ducky 𝓔

I didn't accomplish much to-day. (I mean yesterday) Slept all morning, a couple of hours this afternoon (yesterday) & an hour or so to-night. (last) I keep forgetting it is after midnight. I guess it realy is Monday. If all goes well I'll be home to-morrow (Tuesday). We don't get payed before we leave, so even if I don't get any money one way or another, I'll be home anyway.

I guess the ice must have broken away at the falls because we can hear the water roaring very clearly. I hope I get a chance to go down and look at the falls.

Have you seen Jimmie yet? John got a letter today saying he was in Chatham. He has to be in London to-day I understand, so it isn't likely I'll get a chance to see him.

I must apologize for not answering your last letter in the last one I wrote to you. I forgot all about it.

Yes Sweetheart, I received your paper & thanks a million, but, you bum, you left out the story. But we have lots of storys here anyway.

No, there is absolutely no profit in my canteen.

They fixed the elevator all right, but of course I told you we aren't there now.

Glad you found the kind of pram you wanted Darling, & no doubt they will be able to get a white one for you.

Well Beautiful, I've said about all I can say now so I'll seal it up and mail it.

So-long my Darling & God bless you.
See you to-morrow. All my love, for ever and ever.

X   Don

M.P.O. 203, Niagara Camp, Ont.,
30 January, 1942

Hello My Darling:

Well Sweetheart, here I sit amid a jumble of uncertain thoughts. How is my wife? Am I a Daddy yet? Will I be able to come home for our blessed event? I'm realy not worrying Darling, I'm just anxious. Probably by the time you get this letter the worst will be over; I hope it will Darling.

I was pretty sure I would have word about it to-day. It's nearly nine o'clock in the evening now & there is still time left for a telegram.

I'm still not sure when I'm going away. Monday was the last day I was told, but it may be later & then again they may come & get me out of bed to-night & tell me to get ready.

For the sake of something to write about, I'm on post 32, area 9, on the Welland River. I'm with the Sgt. Maj. this time & we have two other posts to look after. I think this time I will be on the day shift & will be able to sleep the best part of the night.

It was pretty cold here this morning but it warmed up this afternoon & turned out to be a nice day.

I said we are on the Welland R., but we are realy at the junction of the Welland and Niagara Rivers. We can see Niagara Falls N.Y. across the river, the Peace Bridge & the river just before it goes over the falls. I believe we are in one of the Niagara Parks.

It's a nice place & would be very nice in the summer time. To be more explicit, we are right in the town of Chippawa & our sentries patrol the highway to the main street & the main bridge.

Do you remember Hu Fry, he used to have Fry's Taxi Cabs? He has a tourist cabin & trailer camp & gas station right near here.

Very soon I must make a round of the posts & then I think I will be through for the night.

The hut we are in now is just an ordinary old army hut, not as nice as my last one, but it's O.K. I can't expect to have the best accommodations every trip.

Gosh, but my writing is getting more terrible each time I write. I guess I had better "wise-up", & take a bit more time with my letters. I'm still using free stationery. When I get payed maybe I will loosen up & buy myself a writing pad. I also must buy some ink & stamps pretty soon. We get payed to-morrow. I think I have stamps enough for this letter. If I have I will mail this letter when I make my rounds presently.

I got back with my ticket all right last night, without any questions being asked.

Well Sweetheart, I must get on my horse & scamper around my beats.

So-long now Darling & God bless you. All my love Dear, for ever & ever.

X   Don

Michael W Dymond

M.P.O. 203, Niagara Camp, Ont.,
11:20 p.m. Sat. 31 January, 1942.

My Darling Sweetheart:

Well Dear, I haven't received the glad tidings yet. Maybe it's happened already & I haven't heard yet. But I am still anxiously waiting as I have been ever since I got back. I haven't heard anything more about the school I'm going on so I presume I still leave on Monday.

Well Sweetheart, I can't give you a very delightful weather report. It has been raining practically all day & our hut is practically surrounded by water & it is pretty muddy. I have made my rounds already.

I bought a film for the camera to-day, so if it ever decides to brighten up outside I will make use of what photographic knowledge I possess & snap a few snaps. I also bought soap, tooth-paste & stamps.

I have the most money in my pocket now than I've had for a long time, over $20. I wonder how long I can hang on to it. You never know what you are likely to run into on one of these schools. I'll be as economical as possible Darling so that I'll have some left for when I come home the next time. If I don't get home before I leave for St. Johns, & I don't think I will, the next time I'm home we'll be able to go out like we used to. I guess you'll be all better by then, at least well enough to go out. Don't you think so Sweetheart. That is the reason I realy want to save some money. It was such a long time ago that I took you out anywhere. I'm a bit disappointed in myself because I haven't taken you anywhere for such a long time.

I'm stuck for gossip Darling, so I guess this is going to be a very short letter. But I'll write again to-morrow Sweetheart, just to keep as close to you as I can. I like writing to you Darling & it makes me a bit mad when I can't think of anything to write.

So I'll see you to-morrow Sweetheart, & until then so-long & God bless you & I pray that everything is going fine.

All my love to my beloved wife from her faithful hubby,

X   Don

M.P.O. 203, Niagara Camp, Ont.,
11:57 p.m., 1 February, 1942

Hello Gorgeous:

Practically another day is done Darling so I'll finish it with saying "I Love You." And I'll pretend I hear you say you love me. And that starts off a new day.

This watch is sure keeping good time. At midnight it was about 15 seconds fast. It used to loose very slightly, but the last few weeks it has been running perfectly.

I think my pen is running out of ink. I haven't any black ink left, but there is a bottle of red here, so if you have no objections I will fill up with red.

The ration truck brought us out a bundle of old newspapers yesterday & I found a photo of the brigade's inspection soon after we arrived at Niagara Camp. I cut out a couple for you to put in your scrap book, if you still have it. It isn't very clear & I haven't the least idea where I am, but I was there.

It's Monday now of course, & I am supposed to be on my way to-day, though I have heard nothing more about it. Probably the Major will say something about it when he comes later this morning.

I got my things ready this, (yesterday) afternoon, so I'm all set to leave.

Yesterday, -Sunday – was a lazy day for me. I didn't get up until eleven. After dinner & read & got my things ready to move. We had peaches and ice-cream for supper. After supper I went to sleep for a while & went out on my rounds just before ten. It was a bit chilly & snowing, but realy a nice night.

Cpl. Gilhuly took a time exposure of me in the hut this afternoon. I'm wondering how it is going to turn out. He allowed fifteen seconds & the light wasn't any too good. By experimenting like that I will find out just how long to expose the film for different lights.

It's 12:25 now & I realy don't feel a bit tired. But I guess I'll go to bed when I have finished this letter. Might as well get as much sleep as I can.

Nothing ever happens around here. One of the fellows fell down on his rifle & broke it in two, but that is nothing startling, we don't like them anyway.

Pardon me boy, while I roll me a fag!

There is a story on the radio now about a pre-historic sea monster called the "cracken." It has wrapped itself around a submarine & dragged it into a cave I think. The Captain has asked for a volunteer to go out in a diver's suit & make an investigation. He's outside now. He is talking over a telephone to the inside of the sub. Whoops Dearie, the cracken has swallowed the diver & he is talking from inside the monster. He can't be rescued so the Captain orders him to kill himself with his knife & he does. They all come up now with a gun & fire on the cracken, but the cave caves in & all are killed except the Captain & another man. The Captain harpoons the thing and hangs on to the rope.

At last Darling, the news has come & I am so happy! The Major just brought the telegram in & I asked him to send one back. Am I ever happy! I hope to see you to-night.

So-long now & thank God for everything.

Love, Don

MAY, 1943, LONDON, ONTARIO, CANADA, AS IT COULD HAVE HAPPENED TO PHYLLIS...

I think about this stuff all the time. We both knew he would be shipped out sooner or later so having time together, as hard as that is, is so important. Earlier this month Don was in Manitoba, Winnipeg, I think, continuing his training. He doesn't really tell me that much about what he is doing. I guess when he gets overseas, there will be even less. How will we handle that? They sure do a lot of training these days: must be getting ready for something.

Margo is with mom and this little kicky thing in my tummy is keeping me thinking about her. I hope she is being good for her Nana. She will be excited to see me when I get home. She is only sixteen months old but seems to know what is going on. I hope she misses her daddy, too, and remembers him when he comes home. Mom doesn't like to be called grandmother, so Nana is what the kids will be calling her. I guess that's okay.

While visiting Don, Phyllis writes:

Thursday, May 27/43, Hotel Belvedere, London, Ontario, Canada

Don and I arrived here about 12:30 on Tuesday, May 25, put my suitcase in the room, then we went out to get some lunch. He left me at 1pm on the bus corner and I returned back to the room where I did some reading.

He called me at 5 to say he was bringing Lyn up, so the three of us went out to supper, after which we went to the London hotel to have a beer. Stayed there until 9:30 then we returned to the room and we went to bed.

Next morning I had breakfast across the street, then went for a walk, did a little shopping. Had my dinner, then went to a show in the afternoon.

Had supper here in the hotel, then we went to a show, returned and went to bed.

Today, after my breakfast, I walked out Dundas, and went and visited Miss Algeo stayed there for a while, then walked as far as the store with her. Came back up town, did some more shopping and came back cause Don was going to call me at noon, which he did, then I went and had my dinner.

In the afternoon he came up for a while as he was up town, then went back. So he just called saying they would be here in twenty minutes. soo...

They came finally, and we went out for dinner up at Wong's Café, had a nice dinner then went for a beer but it didn't taste right, so thought we would go dancing out at Wonderland. We were a little early so we hitched a ride up to Cobble Stone Inn, the boys had a couple of shots of rye, sat for a while, then left and walked down the Springbank.

The orchestra was playing, but no one was dancing. We had a couple and left for Wonderland again. Stayed there dancing until 11:30, and went to wait for the bus, but it was late, so we got a ride with two boys. And I was tired, even Don didn't want to get up, he didn't leave until 9.

This morning, I had breakfast, walked up town, did a little more shopping and came back here, so here I am, deciding on whether to go for dinner, and later Don is coming up.

Had my dinner finally, came back did a little reading and slept for a while, then Don came so we went out and he bought his shoes, mirror and scissors, then went back to get dressed and he's coming back so we can go out for supper. So I had better get dressed.

Guess I will go back home tonight. Do and I don't.

Don had been in Winnipeg training before returning to the barracks in London, where he and Phyllis, from time to time and as often as possible, were able to spend love's precious, waning moments together. Time was closing in on them. Embarking for England for final preparations before moving to the war's front in France was soon to happen. Although Don may have known this earlier, including the date he would ship out, this wasn't to be shared with families, even loved ones.

By June 1st, Don had travelled to Windsor, Nova Scotia, where preparations for the trip to England were under way. They would leave on June 10th. He and hundreds of other soldiers were making final arrangements: packing, hugging and kissing through the tearful good-byes necessary to buoy loved ones and friends during service abroad which all hoped would be brief. After all, they were heading into a war...a second great war and sadly, after the 1st WW, which was thought to be a conflict to end all conflicts. They all will be missed, and many unsung…'til we meet again.

This is about war and its collateral affect…but the spirit of unconditional love will abide. A play set into action by a few, with the resultant devastation for many. Yet, another war story I did not want to produce. However much we need to remain aware of what war is and what its costs are, in human terms, there needs to be, perhaps, a different approach. The love, acceptance, tolerance and respect for life in all its quarters and of another's soul are what conquer. War: it seems we cannot live with it, or without it.

FOLLOWING IS AS IT
COULD HAVE HAPPENED.
A STORY. 1945

Victory in Europe had been declared. There was much to celebrate and the nation of Canada was preparing to do just that. They had had enough...the world had had enough. Tears shed in fear and loss, were now falling gratefully and generously amid hearty laughter and cheers of reunion. It was over. The radio and all newspapers carried the long awaited tidings: THE WAR IS OVER! The conflict that destroyed countries, indeed much of the world and shattered millions of lives, was done. Six years of death, tears and prayer was enough. Heading home for the weary warrior was paramount and the cleanup in countries now unrecognizable by their own citizens could begin in earnest.

Phyllis and Doreen, a cousin from England spending the war years safely in Canada, were beside themselves. The celebration was starting and what better place to go to be a part of this than to church...your church...Christ Church? A victory dance was planned. Rose had even given a house party for Doreen and all her Canadian friends earlier, as notice of her trip home could come at any time. Their heads bulging with cumbersome, unattractive hair curlers, they danced around the house on Dover Street in high spirits giggling and discussing, like school girls, what they might wear to this dance. They simply couldn't contain themselves.

"Oh my god!" cried Doreen. "It's over. It is all finally over." A sudden sadness overtook her face as she dropped the dress she was holding to herself in front of the mirror in the upper bedroom. She turned to Phyllis as a quiet, regretful smile appeared. "You know I'll be going home...back to England now...don't you Phyllis?"

"Yes," Phyllis said as she pulled Doreen close and hugged her so hard it took her breath away. "Yes, I do, and Don will be coming home soon too," she whispered as tears started to fall. "The kids won't know their dad, she quickly added, but that's okay...it all will be okay. And we'll start over too."

There had been no letters from Don recently and Phyllis had accepted that. She understood there must be much to do at a war's end. Yes, lots of cleaning up, she thought, and yes, all the arrangements necessary for the return of all the boys who had served and survived, including her Donald. She wiped the tears away with the dress she was holding, looked at it and giggled at the silliness, a silliness and laughter that had been overshadowed by years of fear, prayers and hope that the horror would end soon and life could continue once again.

"How will this one look, Doreen?" Phyllis asked holding up her dress. "It's not too bright is it...too cheap like I'll be looking for men to notice me? It won't look like that, will it?"

Doreen hugged her back, even harder. "No! Oh god no! You'll look just fine...you'll look alive and happy. We'll all look alive and happy. And why wouldn't we? The war is over…I'm going home…Donald is coming home…Margo and Michael will have their dad back…Don's mom and dad will be so relieved…it's all going to be so wonderful!"

In their excitement they didn't hear the doorbell ring. Phyllis' mother, Rose Jackson, had answered the door and stood at the bottom of the stairs and called up.

"Phyllis, you had better come to the door."

"Just a minute, mom," came a giggle choked response.

"Phyllis!" Rose called again a little more earnestly, "You'd best come now."

Phyllis dropped the dress she was holding and skipped to the bottom of the stairs with Doreen on her heels. "What, mom?"

Rose pointed to the open front door toward two men in suites standing solemnly on the front porch out of the rain's reach, yet erect and very official. They were members of the local Legion. Phyllis, looking to the men's faces, stared, frozen in her steps. Suddenly she felt her breath leave her body. As her hand cupped her mouth, she thought, it's not Don. She fiddled with her hair trying to make curlers look presentable…ran her hands down her dress pressing out non-existent wrinkles... her heart pounded…her face fell as her lips trembled…tears welled in her eyes.

"Mrs. Phyllis Ethel Dymond?" the man in front asked. "Ma'am, are you the wife of Captain Donald William Dymond?"

Phyllis stared blankly as she attempted to speak. No words came. She couldn't think of what to say. It all quickly became a nightmare. Nothing felt real. It was like she was watching from a distance the whole interaction. She saw herself, but wasn't really there. This wasn't happening.

"Yes, this is Mrs. Dymond," Rose said, as she watched fear overtake her daughter's face.

The man who spoke handed a telegram to Phyllis. "We are very sorry ma'am."

Phyllis took the telegram into her trembling hands, backed up and slumped onto the first step of the stairway. Silence hung heavy in the air. Time stood still. Phyllis heard nothing but her own anxious breath as her heart thumped in her chest. This silence, it seemed, went on forever. Doreen dropped down beside Phyllis slowly wrapping her arms around her kissing her cheek. The salty taste of tears enveloped her lips.

"You'll have to open that, Widdy", Rose said, breaking into tears herself. Rose always called her daughter, Phyllis, by that nickname: Widdy.

As tears feel onto it, soaking it, Phyllis opened the telegram. It, the actual telegram, read as follows:

OTTAWA ONT MAY 7-45
REPORT DELIVERY, 23 DOVER ST CHATHAM ONT.

80743 REGRET DEEPLY CAPTAIN DONALD WILLIAM DYMOND HAS BEEN OFFICIALLY REPORTED KILLED IN ACTION THIRTIETH APRIL 1945 STOP YOU SHOULD RECEIVE FURTHER DETAILS BY MAIL DIRECT FROM THE UNIT IN THE THEATER OF WAR.

DIRECTOR OF RECORDS

851AM8

Suddenly the air became stale, pungent with fear and disbelief. Phyllis choked on the words she read as tears streamed down her cheeks onto the telegram. She read it again. Doreen hugged her tighter as Rose stood stunned by the news. Phyllis' breathing became louder and heavier as she gasped in disbelief. "No! no! no! this is not happening… this can't be happening…Don is coming home…they must be wrong…the war is over…he's coming home," she sobbed. Looking to the opened front door for some explanation, the men, the careworn messengers, had simply disappeared into the rain. Was this a dream, she thought? She read the telegram again and slumped toward the floor and would have fallen if Doreen had not been holding her so tightly.

Time stood still again…silence choked the air again. Phyllis stared at the telegram paralyzed in disbelief. She felt betrayed.

"Where are Margo and Michael?" she asked momentarily as though they had been missing. "Where are they, mom?" she asked looking at her mother.

"It's okay, dear, they are napping...they are okay."

"...and dad? Where is dad, mom?" Phyllis asked disparately looking around the room.

"Dad's in the kitchen, dear. He was here a moment ago, but went back to the kitchen."

"What will I tell them, mom? How will I tell them? I have to call Mammie and Pappy. Oh my god! What will we do? He was coming home...my Donald was coming home!"

Phyllis' lament, and in her own words:

"Many a time I wonder why things turn out as they do. Things go wrong in one's life...romance, marriage, even childhood.

Even mine was sort of everyday sort of life. Could do certain things at certain times, come and go when told...mostly I was afraid of doing the wrong thing, scared of being slapped. Maybe that is why my life turned out as it did.

I was married at 22, my husband, a soldier, been going together for two years, engaged one.

Our married life together was short, just six months we were together before he was moved to different schools of training as he was becoming an officer.

Before he left I became pregnant. He was pleased and used to tease me. I was in a way, but didn't want to start a family so soon. But I was happy anyway, so were the family, his and mine.

I returned to my parent's home where later we made a small apartment at the rear of my parent's home.

My husband came home on different leaves and especially when our baby girl was born.

She really was a cute baby, I guess all parents feel the same and her daddy was quite proud of her, but he had to leave the next day to go back to his camp.

I stayed the usual amount of days then went home feeling happy and glad to have my baby to myself.

Time seemed to pass so quickly when I found out I was pregnant again and my husband was home on his last leave before going overseas.

We had a family dinner, with all our relations. Our little girl was a year old. My husband was overseas when our son was born, which made us very happy. Our family was complete now.

He was over there two and a half years, when near the end of the war he was killed. That really was a shock to us all and I really was in a daze. Our friends were swell, flowers and cards were received."

_____

TO ENGLAND

Donald writes:

There is no point in writing time, date, or place.

My Darling:

I suppose there is no reason why I can't say we are on our third day at sea. This is the first time I've felt like writing – or doing anything as far as that goes.

I haven't missed a meal yet and neither have I lost one – though I have come very close to it.

This morning when I woke up I felt practically normal again. I had a full-course breakfast and felt none the worse for it.

How do you like my writing paper, it's all I could buy.

We have a very nice cabin – the other fourteen fellows and myself. The meals are good.

The Lord only knows when you will get this. No doubt eventually.

What a mess a ship gets into when nearly everyone is sick. tsk-tsk.

The easiest thing to do is sleep. I slept practically all the second day and all that night too.

The ocean certainly is a large place. One consolation – we are only about a mile from land – straight down.

Ten of the chaps sleeping with me are doctors.

I think I may take a bath this afternoon. Sure am getting to feel crummy – I positively stink!

I bought a novel just now for a shilling–"Dead Dogs Bite." I haven't started it yet.

I mustn't write too much now because I'll probably have lots of time to write before we hit land again.

Everyone – including me – seems to be in very good spirits today. This is quite an experience for most of us – and we have a lot to be thankful for – an awful lot when one stops to think things over.

Signing – off for now Sweetheart ___

___On again – Eventually seems to be progressing favourably. We haven't run into any trouble yet.

I bought an eversharp pencil. I wonder how long I'll be able to keep it. I always seem to lose them.

I had my bath and also washed my underwear. I even darned a hole in my sock. Read about half my book. Slept a great deal.

It sure is an education to listen to these MO's talking and arguing.

It must be nearly time for blackout. The public-address system will be announcing it very soon. "Black-out now–Blackout now. Close all port-holes and batten them tightly. I say again – etc."

We really are having wonderful meals Darling. Last evening I had a four course dinner. Soup; lamb, roast potatoes, green peas, mint sauce, rolls; pudding; coffee and a little fish on toast to finish up with. Lovely coffee. Beautifully set table in a large dining room & permanent waiters.

I haven't shaved to-day yet & I guess I won't. But I cleaned my shoes.

Well Sweetheart this has been a bit more conversation. More to come later. Adios—

So again here I am, and lying on my bunk. One has to lie on these bunks, there isn't room to sit up.

Just returned from boat-drill. A bit chilly up there. However, very refreshing. I would think we are getting close to land. Be nice to walk on something solid again.

I finished my little book, standing up on deck just now. It was a murder story. Passed a lot of time away.

I must find out just how I go about mailing this. I want to get it away as soon as possible. I'll try and remember to number my letters so will know if any go astray. This will be no.1. You could do likewise Darling.

Think I'll have a little snooze before lunch. It's 11 now. See you again later. Off!

---On again.

Well Sweetheart, when I run out of information this time, I'm going to bring this letter to a close.

To-day has been a lovely day. Calm and sunny. I think we expect to hit port in the near future.

I just bought a half-dozen chocolate bars in case we miss a meal at some time or other. I also bought four faceclothes, some pipe cleaners. Surprising what can be bought on board. It will be vastly different where we are going, no doubt.

I carried my raincoat on board with me & it certainly has come in useful.

✎ Ducky ✎

I hope you get this soon my Darling. And until my next, may God bless you & Margo and keep you both happy & well until I can be with you again.

My undying love for ever & ever, faithfully your husband,

xx   *Don*

From June 10ᵗʰ to the 17ᵗʰ, 1943, the Empress of Scotland cautiously plowed the Atlantic carrying 4500 frightened, yet eager soldiers to their appointed port of call: Liverpool, England. Beyond the challenges of weather, torturous sea-sickness which affected many inexperienced sailors, the trip was uneventful. Meals were wonderful, conversation no doubt humorous and uplifting even amidst the occasions for the safety of required blackouts. It is for sure that many new friends were made, needed and indeed will be cultivated through the unforgettable and challenging months to come. The loneliness of a soldier in the cacophonous din of war can be deathly unnerving and all were about to face that in the coming months as final training takes place.

Life in Chatham continued, too, with a focus on the war and the hope that it will be short. Hitler had other ideas about that. In some way, everyone was engaged in the war effort. It tends to bring folks together who might not otherwise in the individual business of people's peace time affairs. Unemployment disappeared. All individual effort was war related. Rationing played a major role for all in addition to those busy working away in factories turning out Bren guns, aircraft, tanks and ships. Wages and prices were frozen and many women entered the work force…there were no men.

An 'all for one and one for all' attitude was embraced by the country and each community as the war effort hummed along unimpeded. Winning was the only option.

Donald's training continued in England...

THE ALGONQUINS

The Algonquin Regiment was a complement of a number of other smaller regiments, including the Kent Regiment of Chatham, collected from various areas of Ontario. Canada became the force it was to be on the front in Europe as it grew, trained, served and travelled, coast to coast, from January 1941. On June 10, 1943, the unit embarked on the Empress of Scotland from Halifax harbor as part of a total complement of 4500 troops for readiness training in England. On the eve of the 17th, this ship, the Empress, slipped down the channel, anchoring in the Mersey estuary just outside Liverpool.

Training throughout England continued with intensity, with opportunities for furlough and fun during the latter part of 1943 and up until final preparations were made for Europe. The advance party left for Normandy on the 16th of July, 1944.

NORMANDY: D-DAY, JUNE 6, 1944, THE ALLIED INVASION THAT SAW THE BEGINNING OF THE END OF WWII, HAD ALREADY TAKEN PLACE.

TO THE FRONT

The morning of July 20th saw the loading of three separate troop ships. The following day they idled down the river to the estuary, at which point they anchored for the night due to rough weather. The next day they were into the channel and off to Dover. On the morning of the 23rd they pulled into Portsmouth where they would join up with a larger convoy for the crossing. On the morning of the 24th they were riding a glassy sea to France.

Donald and the Algonquin Regiment sighted the French coast on the afternoon of the 24th. Here, they anchored to wait their turn to land. On the morning of the 25th, the landing on Juno beach went without incident, where they settled down for their first night in France. The next three days were spent getting organized and learning about the beachhead.

Donald had risen quickly through the ranks, achieving the rank of Sergeant in July of 1942 and Lieutenant by March of 1943. His mother Dorothy, and my mother, Phyllis, were both very proud of Donald. No one, however, was more proud of him than his dad, Robert, who served in Egypt with the RAF during WWI and was thoroughly British… ship-shape and Bristol style.

On January 28, 1945, Donald reached the rank of Captain. There had been a number of command changes at that time as heavy fighting was experienced in the Bad Zwischenahn,

Oldenburg area nearing the end of the war. Lives were lost. At the time of command change, Donald was in charge of Support Company "C". His death, at such a point nearing the war's end, was a tragedy felt deeply by both his Company and his family.

Donald was buried in Edewecht Cemetery, Germany, following the war's end. His remains were reburied the following year in Holten Canadian Military Cemetery in Holten, Holland. They remain there to this day.

Lt. D.W.Dymond
The Algonquin Reg't. C.A.O.
1, January, 1945.

My Darling:

You will notice that I got the date right the first time. Usually it takes about a month to get used to putting the right year on.

Well. To-day is the first day of 1945. It is a lovely day. Quite cool, but the sun is shining brightly, and I am sitting here with a glass of real English beer. Of course I would prefer Canadian beer, but English beer is really good when compared with the beer we get in this country.

I found out today that the air mail from England has not been coming over here for a few days so that will account for the fact that I haven't heard from you for some time.

WELL we had our New Years party last night and it went over quite well. A couple of lads were able to procure a few dames, and after all, what's a party without women? We were also very lucky in being able to get a very nice big home to have our party in. It was actually a hunter's lodge. We had a radio and gramaphone to dance to. I managed to get home by five oclock this morning. I figured if I went to bed I would have a hell of a time getting up for breakfast, so I didn't go to bed at all. Anyway, my room is very cold and there was a nice fire until breakfast time, and then had a very nice breakfast.

Before dinner I went to another unit with my CO and had some hot rum punch, and it was very nice. Yesterday we had chicken for dinner and it wasn't bad either. In lots of ways we don't do so badly over here you know. The great trouble is, we can never plan anything very far ahead. As a matter of fact we are always planning ahead. It's the only thing to do. We are quite used to our plans not materializing. We couldn't just go on and never plan anything because then nothing would ever happen.

I didn't really get tight last night, and if I did I was perfectly sober when I arrived home. Notice how I always say home? I was drinking a mixture of cognac and brandy. Quite a mixture eh?

Well, Ducky, the Adjutant is waiting to use the typewriter so I think I had better quit and let him have it.

I have been quite happy on this new years day, and I hope you at home have also been happy.

So-long for now and may God bless you all.

As ever your loving sweetheart.

xxx   Don

                                                       D.W.Dymond

♪ Ducky ♫

Lt. D.W.Dymond,
Alg R. C.A.O. R.H.O.
2 Jan. 1945.

My Darling Phyl:

Here it is the second day of the new year & it isn't a particularly nice day either. Very damp & just freezing. Yesterday morning we actually had some snow. It didn't amount to anything at all. Just enough to say it snowed.

Damn it, I've developed a cold again & and nice cough to go with it. When I went to bed last night I just couldn't stop coughing. I guess the old lady who owns the house heard me because she came up to my room with a pill and a glass of warm water. I don't understand what she says, but I took the pill. And then again this morning before I got up she was back again with another pill & practically two cups of hot milk & sugar. First time since I can't remember when, that I have drank milk.

Now it is getting foggy out. What a weather it is. It seems that the only way to keep warm is to keep moving about. We hardly ever seem to be able to keep a place warm enough to be realy comfortable.

I got myself a new tunic today.

In the house where we now have our mess we found a radio, but it wouldn't work. So a couple of nights ago I fiddled around with it & lo & behold it commenced to entertain us & has been going ever since. It is a cabinet model & works very well. We always have a military wireless set in my office with a loud speaker attached to it. It isn't built for a speaker, just

135

earplugs; but usually we can get one station that is powerful enough to be heard over the speaker, otherwise we use the head phones.

To-day I fancy there should be some Canadian air-mail in. Here's hoping anyway.

Boy, do I feel ugly and irritable. I could bite anyone's head off right now. It isn't often I feel like that.

The mother of a 13 year old girl decided that it was time she told her daughter the facts of life. So she took the kid to one side & gave her the low-down. So the little 13 year old went out to play, & on the corner she met an 11 year old girl.

Said the 13 year old to the 11 year old "I can't play with you"

The 11 year old asked why.

The 13 year old replied, "Because I know the facts of life."

"Oh," said the 11 year old. "I know a few of the facts of life too."

"Alright," said the 13 year old, "I'll ask you a question. Who made you?"

And the 11 year old replied, "Originally, or recently"?

Cute, don't you think? It wasn't very recently that you were made was it?

But it's high time a little fixin' was being done isn't it?

Some of the boys went for a bath this afternoon. I would have gone too but I wasn't in the mood. I sure need one though. Sure would be nice to be able to take a bath just whenever I wanted to.

It's getting along to supper time so I'll finish now. I sometimes wonder if Margo is old enough to understand she has a pop & that he'll be home one day. I know Mike wouldn't.

𝔰 Ducky 𝔠

May God bless you all & keep you happy.
So-long from your sweetheart.

xxx

Don

DWDymond

Lt. D.W.Dymond, Alg. R. C.A.O.
13 Jan. 45

Hello Darling:

I've been a bit busy the last few days, & those days I've missed writing you. It's been quite some time since I used one of these blue forms. My Sgt. just handed it to me as I had no paper to write on. He also says he will give me a stamp. That's Sgt. Benson, better known as Benny. You should see the office I have Darling. Realy modern & up to date, but with one exception, no electric lights. It has lovely neon lights in the ceiling but we must use our Colman lantern. It's a real office in a factory in a little town in Holland. We have been having some cold weather. Not very much snow, but it has been quite cold at times. Haven't heard from you much lately. In the last 3 or 4 weeks I've heard from you 2 letter which arrived about 10 or 12 days ago & both together. You are nearly as bad as me for writing letters, or else the service is on the bum. Oh well, I'm not realy worrying, & you still love me don't you Ducky? And that's the main thing.

My scout car is on the bum again so I'm having a bit of difficulty getting around. Boy, do I hate walking any more.

The kids didn't do too badly for Christmas, did they. From your letter it seems that all went quite well.

That, I'm sure, was not me you saw in a picture pushing a jeep. If I saw the picture I could tell you for sure. Well, sweetheart time to bid you adios. Be a good girl & may God bless you and the kids. My love for you always.

D.W.D   xxx Don.

Lt.D.W.Dymond
The Algonquin Reg't C.A.O.
20 January, 1945.

My darling Wife:

Yesterday I received your letter of 2 Jan. & I can assure you I was realy happy.

It seems such a long time ago that I heard from you. I see the kids are still driving you crazy, so they must be well & as devilish as ever. Even if they are annoying, maybe it's better than having them mope around, because then they wouldn't be all together healthy. There's two ways of looking at this isn't there?

You said Margo was writing a letter to me while you were writing yours, but you didn't put hers in. I suppose I wouldn't understand it anyway.

I know Kitch would be drunk all the time. He couldn't get along if it wasn't for his booze. I never hang onto any bottles Ducky. I don't think I am any more of a drinker than I was in

138

Canada. I still have never been yet so drunk that I passed out or couldn't remember what happened the night before.

I guess you had kind of a quiet New Years didn't you Darling? I was lucky in that we had a dance. I wouldn't say the dance was a roaring success, but we had a good time.

You won't cry so easily when I'm home will you Phyl. The last time I came close to crying was when I said goodbye to you in London. I couldn't get rid of that lump in my throat for a long time. I haven't felt that way since.

Sorry that Peter is gone Darling. Gram will miss him. He was a good dog.

I'm waiting for those pictures Darling. Send them as soon as you can won't you?

We have been having a bit of winter here. I didn't think they realy had a winter here, but they do. I believe once or twice it must have been getting down near zero, or maybe the damp climate made it feel that way. Last night was the first real snow we had & then only about an inch I guess. It packed down hard on the roads and made them real slippery. I was going around corners today like I used to in the car in Canada. I was driving my scout car.

Guess what. Right now and for the next 3 or 4 days I'm adjutant. He's going on leave.

It's a nice night to-night. A slight breeze. A few small clouds, stars, & fairly light. It's clear and the guns sound much closer. To-night they sound something like thunder. And if I was close enough or it was darker I could see the flash....

...And now here it is 2 pm the next day, Sunday. So far to-day I have been fairly busy. It always takes longer to do a job when you aren't used to it & you have to use the old bean to figure things out. But so far everything has gone fine.

This morning it was quite cold. Must have been about zero. Everything was completely white with frost. It was very pretty outside.

Our monthly liquor ration arrived to-day. Did well this time. A bottle of Scotch & a bottle of Gin. Just had a slug of Scotch. Would you care for one Dear? It's quite good. But due to the fact I'll have to keep my whits about me, I must take it easy.

Now it is Tuesday & hell or high water I'm going to finish this letter to-night.

The Adj. should be back to-night so my duty in this office should cease then. I really have more or less enjoyed the job. I wouldn't mind it for a few more days.

I trimmed my moustache a little while ago. It had a few ragged bristles hanging out of it, but now it's nice and neat again. I'll bet you'd like to see this moustache of mine. It's developed quite a bit since you last saw it, but it is by no means ungainly. I think you will like it.

Think I'll buy some stamps & start using a few air mail forms.

It's a bit chilly in here because the fireman couldn't get the fire to burn all afternoon. There is a new fireman here now & I hope he succeeds. Coke doesn't burn well in a small fire.

I don't think I would be very efficient in an office. I just can't seem to keep it tidy. My desk always seems to be littered with paper.

Bob Watson, Ethel's brother sent me a few hundred cigarettes from England a couple of days ago. I had just finished my last pouch of Canadians too.

❡ Ducky ❡

My bottle of whiskey is gone, & I didn't get at all tight. Now I'll have to wait another month. But who cares, I don't.

Well, the fire is going.

I talked the Q.M. into a new pair of trousers yesterday & he sent them to me to-day. Aren't I lucky? Got to keep my appearances up you know.

Looks like the fire is realy going to burn. Gee, I sure could go for a real dance. I feel like a party. Do I look like one?

Come on fire...BURN!!!

I'd better clean this place up before the boss arrives, he'll wonder what happened.

Are the Russians ever going to town. Hope they get stopped before they run into us. I'd better make some signs & put up so they'll know when to stop.

Thanks for Fred's address. I'll try & get in touch with him.

How's your kid sister behaving herself?

Thanks for the lovely kiss in your last letter Darling. Realy smells nice. Just reminds me of your kisses. I could just feel your lips on mine when I opened it. What one of your kisses wouldn't do for me now. It would be just like heaven. I wouldn't worry about a fire at all.

By the way, it's still burning. I can start to feel the heat leaking back into my blood stream.

Be a good girl. I hope I don't have to say that as I know you always are. Just be as happy as you can.

So-long sweetheart & may God bless you all.

As ever your sweetheart.

xxx   Don

A letter from Phyllis that survived…

Wed, Jan, 24/45

To My Darling.

Repeat after me. "Je te aimes beaucoup." That will give you something to do; to figure that out, that is, if you remember your French & being over there you should have brushed up on it.

Anyway if you can't you know I do anyway, don't you dear.

You made me very happy dear this week. First, I received a $100. bond from you on Monday, then this morning 2 letters, which were very welcome. First I've had in 3 weeks. You said you haven't received any from me, but you will cause I have been writing, so you should be getting some soon. Have you received your Xmas box yet. You didn't say in your letter of today, but here's hoping you have. Boy, am I glad this day is nearly over, these kids of ours really got me down today, especially Mike, he needs two to take care of him. The other day he knocked over Mom's trilight lamp & broke the reflector, then the next day he reached two dishes of pudding, that was on a tray on the sink board, & they went crashing to the floor, what a mess, later in the day, it was a glass, & the next a plate. Today no dishes, but enough trouble, that made me glad to put him to bed, & Margo did nothing else but cry. Talk about your nerves. If I keep talking like this, you'll be nervous in a different way. Tonight, Mom has gone to play Bingo, & Doreen is playing basketball just what we used to do in the good old days. She plays on the

Church team with Mrs. Watson & Willie, coaching them. The Goddards are still going strong, with different players. Jo Down, & Ada (Ellis) Graham, guess she is their top player. Lou Osman, & others, & the other day Lou asked me to come out and play, but I can't get away very well & I'm getting to stiff and creaky. (Oh me) Need you to fix me up, & I guess you need me to warm your nose up being it is cold, & cool George off. This is from your letter dated Dec 30, you say you have no complaints, & feeling fine, which I am thankful, cause I do want you all in one piece so I can feel your two arms around me tight. I see you have bought some shirts and stuff. Can't wait, I know, but a box is on its way with some more clothing in it. So watch out.

Can't get your pen, silly, your just too lazy to walk over and get it. (ha). My room is nice and warm, sometimes I have to through my top cover off, would you like some of the heat, me, included.

The war doesn't look too bad, but I don't listen to very much news, gives me the willies. A news man comes on at 5 to 9 pm. For 5 mins, in fact he is on now, & he gives a lot of news. I like to hear him, & one that comes on at 2 in the afternoon, which is very good. Those are the only two I listen to & the paper don't give very much.

I have an idea you are with the 2nd Army & they have been very busy lately, so I follow them in the paper.

I certainly would like to go to a dance with you Darling, & all dressed up. I'm always dreaming like that just waiting for the day when we can go out together & I would give anything if you did tap me on the shoulder & ask for the next dance. Think I would stand there with my mouth open and then cry.

Went to the I.C. a week ago to the dance, & they had an orchestra from Windsor, which was grand, but they didn't arrive until 11 & supposed to be at 9. They got stuck in the snow near Tilbury. Also, they quit at 12, but beings they were late, we danced until 1 am. Had a pretty good time, but much rather have you so I could show off with my husband.

You continue to say you are somewhere, maybe B. or H. but you are not in Germany. Thank God.

Lets see what you say in your other letter. Yes dear you are improving by getting the date right. Always knew you had it in you. (tsk)

You are drinking some beer, just wait Ducky, we will have some beer when you come home. We always have some in. Glad you had a party, & as you say, what is a party without dames, & I say the same about men.

So, sorry you had to cut your letter short, couldn't the Adjutant wait for a while, so you could finish your letter, or am I kidding.

Here's a joke…

A Sarg was ordered to have the Wacs give a kit inspection. So he did & told the officer. He looked them over & was surprised to see them stripped from the waist up.

So he said, I ordered kit inspection.

A woman went to see her doctor cause she wasn't feeling well, & he told her she was having too many children. So he asked her if she liked bananas, & she said yes. He said, eat them.

Well, Sweetheart, guess I have told you all I can think of right now. You know tomorrow being Thursday, I will drag the brats up to the Dymond's flat. I mailed those long letters to you. Pappie gives them to me for mom to read, then I mail them.

So, My darling, as you say, may God keep you safe & happy for me, Margo & Mike & hope we see you in the New Year especially the kids.

This time, I really mean it signing off, so with All my Love as ever in your dreams.

Phyllis, Margo, Mike
xx   xx   xx

Here's some more of Doreen's French.
"Vous etes un petit devite."
Plus de plus cette Coeur de meme confesseur.

Lt. D. W. Dymond,
B.H.Q. Alg. R. C.A.O.
27 Jan 45
My Darling Phyllis:

The weather to-day is very much like Canadian weather. Not to cold & a lot of snow. A bit dull but realy not dreary. Last night it was quite nice out. It was bright & snowing lightly. I could picture you & I walking arm & arm, going home from the show or a dance, & sometimes stoping to put my arms around you and kiss you. I can feel your cold cheeks on mine & the look of love in your eyes. I think that certain qualities in a fellow sort of go a little dead when he is almost completely isolated from friendly feminine life. I don't think I've changed at all since I left you, except that I am a bit older. I'm just as silly &

devilish as I ever was. But I need you Darling to add something to my everyday life that I can't get from the soldiers I live with. Mind you they are all good fellows, & we get along swell. Jimmy looks after my things quite well, the cook gives us good food, I always have a car to go where I want to. My clothes are the best and enough of them. I have a doctor & a dentist free. I don't work so very hard & I always have some money – even if there is nothing to spend it on. I have many privileges. But what I haven't got, & what I need & want more than anything else is you Phyl. It won't be long now. It doesn't seem at all right that you are my wife & I have a family & yet I must be away from you so long. It won't last for much longer & then we can share each other's happiness. So-long for now Darling & may God bless & keep after you. As ever your Sweetheart.

xxx   Don

Lt. D.W.Dymond
B.H.Q. Alg. R. C.A.O.
28 Jan. 45.

My Darling:

    Here it is Sunday night & it is quite cold out. I'm sitting at the Adjt. Desk & he's toasting his shins by the stove. Like to meet Bob? he's not a bad guy. (The following is in Bob's own handwriting)

This hubby of yours should know too! I knew Don when he was a curly headed little fellow living next door; he was sweet & gentle then! In fact he hasn't changed a great deal. He spends most of his time at his modern office saying "no" to civilian requests. Yes even to cute little blondes! Seriously for a moment, I should be pleased as the dickens if you ever drop up to London drop in & visit my wife – better drop her a note first – she wanders around the country at times spending the family fortunes. Her address is 20 Rathgan St – her name is Rene – her phone is Fairmont 1457J – I'll drop her a line myself & introduce you – au revoir for now – all the best – Bob.

I've censored the above so I guess it is O.K. But I bet you don't agree with him saying that I am still sweet and jentle. I often think of the time I came home from Terrace to go to O.T.C and you had left to go to a dance at the T.C. I dashed in the house & there was Margo sitting on Gram's knee, & she looked at me as if she didn't know who I was, as she probably didn't. I just asked where you were & turned around to leave & Gram said "well, aren't you going to kiss your daughter?" which I did in a very stupid manner, & dashed out to catch you. Remember how surprised you were to see me? It took about two blocks for you to be convinced that it realy was me. But it was, wasn't it? Many little things like that I think of now & then. Gives me a nice feeling when I think about those sort of things. Well Darling, time to say good-night, & may God bless you all. As ever your faithful Don.

xxx
D.W.Dymond

Michael W Dymond

Capt. D. W. Dymond,
B.H.Q. Alg. R. C.A.O.
31 Jan. 45.

Hi Ya Pal:

See anything peculiar about the heading. Now I hope you're satisfied you rascal you. To-day I'm wearing my nice new rubber boots that I had issued to me a few days ago. The weather changed last night & now the snow has practically disappeared & it has been raining. Received a letter from you yesterday. I'll run upstairs and get it. The sooner I get those new snaps the happier I'll be Ducky. I don't wish discussing armies and commanders in letters, so if it is O.K. by you I won't say anything about it. I guess by the time you receive this, the mail situation will have improved, I hope. No one seems to get any mail from me. Oh Dear! Received 300 Winchesters from Mrs. C.D. Luff yesterday. Was glad too, because I've been smoking Limies. Boy, am I hungry. Wish someone would come and let me eat. – now I've had it. Boy, does the wind blow here. One day it was realy blowing, so hard that one of the hens in the back yard had its rear end into the wind & laid the same egg six times! The Q.M. is here and we are trying to talk the Adjt. into letting us both go on leave to England together. We're having a hard time to convince him that it would be for the good of everyone, including the English gals. But he doesn't seem to believe us. We'll have to work on him some more. Have you been doing any skating Ducky? If I had my skates on I'd try though I'll bet I'll be awfully wabbly. Next winter Margo will be able to learn to skate won't she? And she'll be three years old day after tomorrow. Doesn't time fly?

*Well, Darling, it's time to sign off. May God bless you all &
remember I love you. As ever your sweetheart. xxx Don.*

D.W.Dymond

Capt. D.W. Dymond
C. Coy. Alg. R. C.A.O.
3 Feb. 45.

Darling Phyl:

As you will notice I have another change of address. I
realy get around don't I?

Believe it or not, at present I have a company all of my own.
Actually, I'm 2i/c (second in command). But if nothing else it's
an increase in pay - $1.50 a day. So far I like it, but these are
the good & bad in all these jobs. I haven't electric lights, but
the coal oil lamps aren't too bad. We have a wireless set that we
can get the odd program on. The food is good, & so far the cook
has been feeding me too much. So far the room has always
been warm. I spend most of the night awake. Beside the lads
in Coy. H.Q. there are four telephones to relieve the monotony.
You know, I have another cold. That's three in almost as many
months. Getting to be a nuisance. And I always get a dickens
of a cough with them. But I don't feel at all sick, & in a couple
of days my cold will be pretty well gone. The last few days
have been like spring. The sun was shining to-day & I spent
some of my time firing my pistol at small turnips floating
in a stream & also trying to cut down a cement gate post
with my rifle. We have to keep our eyes open these days as we

might accidently shoot some Russians!! They sure are going great guns aren't they? And I hope they keep it up. All we're interested in these days is, how far are the Russians from Berlin. That city must be an awful wreck, Ducky. I could use a few more pairs of socks. I haven't a large supply & it takes so long to dry clothes in this country that sometimes I wear the same pair for three days, which isn't long but I don't like doing it, particularly in wet weather when I wear rubber boots. I could also use a few razor blades occasionally. But I am far from complaining. I realy can't say that I lack anything. I love you Darling, & give the kids a good night kiss each night from their daddy. Good night sweetheart, & for you all my love.

As ever your adoring,

xxx Don

D.W.Dymond

Capt. D.W.Dymond
C. Coy. Alg. R. C.A.O

My Darling Phyllis:

The eve of another day. This cold of mine seems to have lodged in my head & it's giving me a bit of a headache the last couple of days. Not serious though like I used to get. I have electric lights again. My office is now in a pub, a pub except that there isn't even an indication of a drink, not even water. It's a good thing it isn't cold as we have no fuel for the stove. The Sgt. Major is lying on the bed beside me, snoring. The clerk is clerking at the table in the next room. The signalers are sitting in front of the wireless, giggling, and one is playing solitaire, while the company runner is leaning over his shoulder helping him. Outside, everything is very quiet, except for the occasional dull boom of a gun. The stars are shining but it is still quite dark. There are no civilians around because they must be in their home at 6 pm until 7 am. That is the situation at present. So until the next time, so-long & may God bless you & Mike and Maggie. As ever your adoring hubby.

xxx   Don

Capt. D.W.Dymond,
C. Coy. Alg. R. C.A.O.
11 Feb. 45.

My Darling:

Here it is Sunday nearly all gone again.

This morning I went to Church pde. & took Holy Communion. This afternoon I went to a show in a real theater. The first real theater I've been in since England. The picture was "Broadway Rhythm," in Technocolour. I enjoyed it. I'll be sure & see that picture you were talking about if it comes & I'm able to go.

I'll bet Margo does look cute in her little plaid skirts. Wish I could see her myself.

Still having the cold weather eh? We've had no more here. It's healthy when it's cold even if it is uncomfortable at times.

Those pictures are not me, Darling. Sorry to disappoint you. I guess they do look like me though.

So you wouldn't mind my bum close to yours eh? It would be more than just my bum close to you. It would be George inside you trying to hit bottom & boy how he would try & I'll bet he'd make it too.

That's a shame to cut down that nice big tree. Guess it must have been pretty old & maybe not quite safe.

I had a letter to-day & yesterday from you & they were both nice long ones too. I know that I am the only one that can realy make you but it's nice to hear you say so.

Hope you are able to get a picture of you and Mike and Margo for me. I sure need one.

This old war is still progressing favourably as far as I can see Ducky, & it is going to last for a while yet. But as I said before, the end does seem to be in sight. We are either holding our own or making progress on all fronts.

Gee, but there's not much to talk about. At present I'm sitting on two Jerry tin – petrol tins – in an office where there are no electric lights. Something wrong with the lights anyway – by the light of one of those pressure lights. A couple more of the chaps are writing letters & two more are playing crib.

Remember my little Jeep I got for Xmas. Well, I gave it away to a couple of little Dutch kids. Guess you won't mind. They have had nothing new or different in a long, long time.

The last few nights have been very long. Nothing to do realy. Just a matter of being here. Oh well, I suppose things will brighten up one day, & the long evenings will be spent in one way or another.

❦ Ducky ❦

So-long now Ducky, & may God bless you all. Once again I say I love you as I always will.

Keep smiling. Your sweetheart,

xxx   Don

Saturday, Feb. 10/45

To the one I Love.

With all my heart, & very proud of it to, especially now, that you have a new handle to your name.

That really is swell, you deserve it anyway, how do you like it, or does it make any difference anyway. I love you just the same anyway, no matter what you are.

I just had to spank Mike's hand, as he pulled the cloth on the table, & upset the desk with a plant in it, water all over.

He makes up his mind to touch anything and he does it.

Thursday, I took my three airmails up to P. & M. but they had two from you dated 27 & 28, so I let him read the one of mine dated 31 & he was pleased to know you had it, way he spoke, he seemed to know about before. Did you?

Had to fix up Mike, as his pants where right down to his knees.

Say, Darling, can you have a picture done of you for me, want to see if you have changed, & if I still love that dear face.

And my dear husband, I didn't find out until Thursday up at P. that you received your xmas box, cause you said in his letter that someone swiped your jeep, well you just get it back, that was to be a keepsake, & tell that somebody off or I won't

153

send you any more boxes. Oh me! That Bob, did you know him before & was it in London.

Yes dear, I often think of that night especially when I go down to Nora's, & remember that you met me half way. Just wish it could happen again. In your other letter of 27 you say you are a little older, well, you & me both, but I act silly sometimes, guess we do need each other to liven us up. Just hope you are right Darling, in saying we will be together soon, just can't wait, so we can go for a walk out to one of our favourite spots.

There isn't anything to do here, only go to the show, & lunch after, and that gets stale.

When we are together we certainly are going stepping.

Margo just asked me if I was writing to Daddy. I said yes, & telling him what a cry baby you are & she laughs.

Well, sweetheart, just wish you were here, so I could kiss and hug you so much to say. I'm very happy for you in your promotion, & love you so much, as you know I do.

So, until we are together once again. Ever yours as always.

X

Phyllis, Margo,
xxxx Michael

Saturday, Feb. 17/45.

Dearest Don:

Just feel like writing, don't know whether I'm in the mood for it, but just for you dear, just feel blue & droopey. I have an excuse for that, cause I have my friend, but that doesn't mean I don't want you, cause I do very much.

If we could hold each other close & don't say anything, just feel each other close together, that would just be heaven, don't you think so dear.

That damn Nora, she is always eager to go to the I.C. dances, but when the last minute comes, she won't go. I am used to her blowing her trumpet about going, so I just let her rumble off, cause I know her, so I didn't go. Called Phyl I. up, but she has joined the badminton club, & likes it & said if I couldn't get anyone to go, she would go with me. But I can't call her again, so I felt so blue, went to the show by myself. But just wished you where with me. So, last night I took Doreen cause she has been good to watch the kids for me, & it had a short picture of D. Day to Brussels, & it was very good. Showed a lot of the boys in action & on the move, & one riding a M. C. thought it was you, but never showed the faces clearly, & some whizzing by in jeeps, trucks & tanks. Some scenes where a mess.

Before I answer your last airmail, I was going to write to the fellow Bob's wife, but what is their last name please. I do not know. Thought you told me in one of your letters, but can't find it. So please inform me & I will write. Do you think that a good idea? If you think so, say so. Don't keep me in suspense. Dear, we are going to have our pictures taken, for you, on Wed, but they won't be done until end of April. Long time eh? But I will send you a proof, so that will give an idea. Also, think I will have my hair done, I'm so sick of it this way. Enough of this, see what is in your letter, yes, I see your address is changed again. Yes, the Russians are going strong, & getting places, but can we trust them? Pappie don't think so. So, you want some socks, there is a pair in the last box I sent you soon should get. But I will send you some more, also some blades.

The kids here are wrecking the place. Guess will put the kettle on for dinner as it is 11.30.

Now it is 1.30. Dinner & dishes are done, the sun is shining & looks nice & brisk out. The last two days it has been thawing, & the streets are slushy, & there goes my stockings. Well, Sweetheart, it is two years since we were in London buying your officer's suit, remember?

My last page & also running out of news, have to get Margo and myself ready to go uptown and get my papers, etc. & go in and see Mammie.

Being tomorrow is Sunday, it is my turn for church, so will sing to you dear.

Until then my Darling. May God keep you safe in your new duties.

Remember I love you dearly.

Yours forever,

Phyllis, Margo
& Michael

X   xxxxx

🪝 Ducky 🪝

Capt. D.W.Dymond,
Alg. R. C.A.O.
20 Feb. 45

Hello Ducky:

Fancy me being here?

Believe it or not I'm in dear old London, on leave.

Generally speaking it's been quiet, but I don't mind that realy.

I'm sort of wondering how I am going to mail this. We are supposed to use

Military mail channels, but I don't know what we're supposed to do on leave.

Since I've been here the weather has been realy wonderful. Real spring

weather.

I hope my aunts and uncles don't know I'm here because I haven't been to

visit them. Bet mum won't like that when I tell her. Oh well.

About two more hours & I'd be pretty well pickled. I drank just about all the

beer I could plus a scotch & a few rums. Guess I must be getting immune.

I'm mailing a present for Mike & Margo Ducky. At least a girl I know here

in London is going to mail them to you for me.

I met her when I was in England before.

I can't remember whether I mentioned her to you before or not.

Jack McLeod arranged a blind date for me one evening for a dance in the mess

& she is very nice, as English girls go.

She has a son 3 ½ years, & her husband is a prisoner of war.

She more or less persuaded me to buy these presents.

Hope you like them Darling.

I had nine days all told over here, but it sure went fast. If nothing else it's a

change.

Hope you don't mind me sending these along to the kids the way I have. It's

just simpler that's all.

Anyway, I'm behaving myself.

So-long Darling & may God bless you all.

As ever your sweetheart,

xxx   Don

                                         D.W.D.

❦ Ducky ❦

Capt. D.W.Dymond,
C. Coy. Alg. C.A.O.
28 Feb. 1945.

Hello Darling:

About time I was writing again, isn't it? Probably by now you have received my letter I wrote in England. I think I remember pretty well what I wrote though I remember at the time I had had a few drinks. Anyway, I'm back at the old grind again. I can't tell you what the score is here, but you read in the papers what the Canadian Army is doing. I saw a very nice picture on the way back from England, "The White Cliffs of Dover" & curiously enough I saw it in Calais. Calais is a very desolate looking town. Hardly a house that isn't damaged in some way. Darling, I don't know if you've seen that picture, but when I saw it that was the first time since when I said good-bye to you in London that I had that nasty lump in my throat. I didn't cry, but felt that way. I don't know whether it was just the good acting in the picture or the mood I was in. My leave in England was very quiet. I didn't get tight once. Saw a few shows & went to a dance. Had at least 8 hours sleep a night. That doesn't sound like a very exciting leave does it for a chap that's been over in Europe for 7 months. Hope you like the present Joan is sending you for me, & I also hope you don't mind her sending them for me. Generally speaking I don't care much for English girls, but she's quite nice. I'm doing fine Darling. Give my love to all at home & may God bless and guide my little family. Received snaps but I want a good one of you. As ever with love Don.

XXX

D.W.Dymond

Capt. D.W.Dymond,
C. Coy. Alg. R. C.A.O.
2 Mar 45

My Darling:

To-day is a very nice day except that it has turned a bit cold & quite a wind blowing. I have some of your letters here Ducky, that have accumulated. Received both Valentines. I'm ashamed of you, teaching my daughter to cuss – tsk, tsk. Hope you made the I.C. dance and enjoyed it. The snaps are quite good Darling but I realy want a good one of you. You were good in the snaps but too far away. I'll send you a picture of me. I do like your hair Darling – just perfect. I think that a very good idea of yours, to go on a second honeymoon when I come home. I would like you as a secretary but you wouldn't be able to work in that nice office because we aren't there, & I'm sure you wouldn't like it here. I haven't got a vehicle of my own anymore, though I manage to get around if I need to. That was a lovely box you sent me Darling. I'm wearing the wide part of the wrist strap you sent me. I'm going to save the shirt for a special occasion. There's all the difference in the world in Canadian and English chocolate. I don't bother to eat the Limy stuff. Haven't worn the collar pin yet. At present I'm wearing my long underwear, but soon it will be warm enough to wear the shorts. The little soldier was cute & the rest of his broken foot came off. When I was in London I bought myself a wallet, the other one was worn out. But everything you sent was realy swell Darling, & I love you for it all.

I see my children are becoming drunkards very early in life. Isn't that terrible? My – my!

Well, it's dinner time so I must finish up & go eat. Never lose my appetite you know. Just as healthy as ever. Boy, are you going to take a beating when I come home, or maybe it'll be me what'll take a beating. I'll probably wear out before you. It seems that I was always the one who quit first. Right? Guess I just couldn't take it. Well, Sweetheart, be seeing you soon, I hope. So-long now & may God bless you all. As ever your sweetheart,

D.W.D.   xxx Don

Capt. D.W.Dymond,
The Algonquin Regt. C.A.O.
5 Mar. 45.

Hello Sweetheart:

Enclosing the receipts for war bonds for you to look after. You can take better care of them than I can. I guess you haven't received the bonds yet. That's what there is to come anyway.

All seems to be going as planned Darling.

There is still nothing to tell you realy.

You might be interested in knowing that I'm in Germany, but there is realy no thrill to it nor anything strange about it.

As much as I've seen the Fatherland is taking an awful beating. It's practically impossible to find a house that is intact. The majority are demolished or very nearly so. There will certainly be a lot of rebuilding to do when it is all over. It's sort of nice to know that all the houses in Canada are standing & that there will be a home to come to. There are millions of people here who won't have a house of their own for years.

I don't mean to pester you with the dreary side of life, but you can see that Jerry is certainly taking quite a beating. And of course Canada is losing some men too.

Have just been reading the B.B.C. news that I sec type out every day for us & as far as our W. front is concerned, it all looks good.

Dinner time again & there realy isn't much I can tell you. Just listen to the radio & read the papers about the Canadian Army.

Be good Darling & may God bless you all. I love you.

For ever
xxx Don
D.W.Dymond

Ducky

Capt. D.W. Dymond
Sp. Coy. Alg. R. C.A.O.
17 Mar. 1945

Hello Darling:

Yes! Once again I've had a change. I'm back in support Coy again. This time I'm Sp. Coy Commander. I took C Coy into action & now here I am. I realy get around don't I? Haven't written for quite a while. War you know. Received the letter with the proof of your picture. I think it could be better Darling. Probably the other one is better. Hope to send you a picture of me someday soon. I'm doing fine. We are having a party tomorrow night. I'm now mess secretary. I didn't want the job, but I was just told I was secretary & that's all there is to it. Damn it! I seem to be getting another cold in my chest. I've had too many colds this winter. Oh, what's the difference. I now have a Jeep again. It's practically new too. So I get around again. At present I'm living in the rectory of a Church. I have a nice feather mattress on a real bed. Sure sleep good. Where is Harry Parker, Darling? He's not with his unit. And what is Shirley doing?

I notice in the paper that the Algonquin Reg't have been fighting with the Canadian Army in Germany. Time to say so-long now Sweetheart & I love you so much. May God bless you all. As ever your adoring hubby.

xxx Don

DWD

Michael W Dymond

Capt. D.W.Dymond,
Sp. Coy Alg. R. C.A.O.
28 Mar 45

My Darling:

My most humble apologies for not writing for a few days.
The truth is. I've been busy because I have a large Coy. Many
bits of administration etc. to look after, and also I've been
trying to make the best of my social activities. We've had a
bit of a rest & 2 or 3 parties & enjoyed it all. I've enjoyed myself.
I've been secretary of our mess for a couple of weeks now & that
has kept me a bit busy. I have received quite a lot of mail in the
last 2 weeks & if I tried to answer it all would take too much
time. So I'll stick to here Jack as there isn't enough paper to
do more. I've been behaving myself, & that's something isn't
it? We have been having wonderful weather lately. No rain at
all & the sun has been shining often. Hope it keeps up so that
our vehicle can keep rolling & Jerry will be licked & I'll be home
that much sooner. To-night I hope to be in bed by 9 pm, so I can
catch up on my sleep.

So remember I love you truly and soon I'll be coming home
& that you will realy have your hands full looking after me
besides Margo and Mike. So-long Darling & may God bless
you all. As ever your adoring Sweetheart. DWD xxx Don.

ॐ Ducky ॐ

Capt DW Dymond
Sp Coy Alq R CAO
13 Apr 45

My Darling:

Today is Friday the 13ᵗʰ and it has been a very nice day. The sun has been shining and it has been quite warm. Tonight it is getting very damp and cold but we have lit a fire in this room and I think it is going to be nice and warm. They burn a lot of peet in this country. It doesn't give a tremendous heat but it is better than nothing and the weather isn't cold at all.

By the way how do you like this note paper? Pretty isn't it? Yesterday I received a box of Laura Secord chocolates from Mrs. Solomon, and they are realy good. They were sent to me congratulating me on my third pip.

It was quite a while ago that I typed a letter to you wasn't it? It is just for a change.

It is nearly time for our ten o-clock snack. Probably fried egg sandwiches to-night, and coffee. For supper to-night I had fried chicken and potato chips and stewed rhubarb, all cooked up by my Sgt Maj. He is realy good. And we have lots of fun together at times.

Well, Jerry is still fighting. But now it all seems to be drawing to a close, I hope. It's kind of funny in a way how Jerry continues to fight on. He is so broken up and the commanders of these groups are afraid to quit because they don't know what is going on in other parts of Germany. They are sort of in a tight spot.

There should be lots for me to talk about but I just can't seem to think of what to say. We haven't been through a particularly wealthy part of Germany, but I can assure you that the people are far from being starved. They have lots to eat and lots of clothes and they seem to have lots of everything else, except for petrol and a few odd things like that. But they have looted the whole of Europe it seems and they have been living in luxury. But I am afraid they are a little bit disappointed now. They have lost a lot of their homes, and for just such foolish and little things. Here's an example: The other day a sniper took one shot at me. We spotted him as he was headed for a farm building, so we fired at the building and burned it down. It all seems so fruitless doesn't it? And all that has to be rebuilt again too and it will take years and years to do it. And look at the thousands or millions of men. Women and children they have lost. And we have lost a lot too.

The other day all the officers put in ten guilders with a guess as to when this war would be over and the one that guesses the nearest to the right date takes all the money and gets a seven day leave. That should be about 350 guilders which is about 125 dollars. A fellow could have quite a leave on that much money couldn't he? I was very optimistic and guessed at the 17th of April. I don't care about the money or leave as long as the war is over and I can come home to you and the kids.

Gee, I hope I can get a bath pretty soon. I realy need one badly. I started to scratch myself to-day. I've got itchy nuts. Did you ever have itchy nuts? It's embarrassing as hell because you have to keep scratching yourself. Wish you were here to scratch me Ducky. But your chance will come, one of these days.

Well Darling it is now eleven o-clock and I feel kind of sleepy so I think I will close now and go to bed.

Good night now and may God bless you all. As ever your adoring sweetheart,

xxx Don

D.W.Dymond

Capt. D.W. Dymond,
Sp. Coy. Alg. R. C.A.O.
23 Apr. 45

My Darling:

It is now 12:15 in the morning & I'm here in my office. My office changes practically every day, but every house I go into I call my office.

I'm listening to the battle over my wireless set & also occasionally answering the phone.

Everything seems to be going quite well. This war looks as if it is going to be fought to the bitter end. It looks as if we'll have to either kill or capture every German to finally finish things up.

From the general news I would think that the Americans and Russians are pretty nearly linked up. Getting to Berlin isn't going to finish the fight though.

Sorry my mail hasn't been very plentiful lately & I hope to be able to do better in the future.

Received the snaps Ducky & they are grand. You look as beautiful as ever & the children have realy grown wonderfully.

Funny thing, I've developed another cold. They are never realy bad & don't stop me in any way from working. But I always get a cough & it's damn annoying.

Saw Pat Coulter a short time ago & thanked him personally for seeing you safely home from London.

I've only been in one place in Germany where there were electric lights. Mostly we use candles or coal-oil lamps. I could use a lamp from the battery of my jeep, but it's a bit hard on the juice.

I have a nice pair of wool lined air force boots. I think they would be nice and warm in winter time. Wish I had had them last winter.

The weather lately has not been too bad. Gradually getting warmer and very little rain.

Just paused to have a piece of bread and syrup. Boy – could I sleep right now. My eyes are tired.

Now it's the next day and I am waiting for dinner. Then after dinner I'm moving to a very big house that has nothing but walls & only parts of them.

To-day is a very nice day. The sun is shining. Dinner is here.

I was watching Spitfires dive-bombing Jerry just now. What a noise they make, & do they go.

Well, Sweetheart, to you all the very best – a few 'moaning minnies" just came in – God bless and take care of you.

Your loving hubby,
xxx Don

❧ Ducky ❧

11:30 pm Monday, April 23/45

Dearest One:

Here I go writing to the one I love with all my heart. Haven't wrote to you in the last few days, just can't seem to concentrate on writing, & it is not because I don't think of you, or care, cause you are always on my mind, in everything I do and see.

Just finished a piece of bread & jam & a glass of milk, so felt in the mood for writing you, so here I am, cigarette and all.

I went to the show tonight all by myself & saw a good picture, "Winged Victory," & some of the scenes brought back memories of you and me. When I used to visit you at the barracks, kiss you good night outside the gate, you go one way, me the other, those were hard to take, when you couldn't have your husband when you wanted him & not even now. (period.) (ha), go to a dance, & hold me close, & we would sing or hum the piece of music. Right now I could love you to pieces. Couldn't you. Sometimes Darling, I just want you so bad, even putting my hand between my legs & squeezing tight feels good, but much rather have yours. This may not sound right for me in my letter, but you know how I feel, don't you, Darling, & I the same for you. Think that is all we need to buck us up, some days I'm no good. The war news looks pretty good, but I know it will be a long time yet before we are together again, & I know you would like to be with your two children, (did I say two). Can you imagine you are the Daddy of two kids, sometimes I can't. But here's hoping and praying it won't be very much longer.

169

Guess Doreen will be going home soon, she just has to be ready for short notice, 2 days, 2 weeks, 2 months. She is all thrilled. Her people in their last letter said they haven't heard from you, in fact don't know much about you, they thought maybe you didn't like them. Do you? I know you aren't much on letter writing, who is.

Marg McVeigh was sitting in front of me tonight with a man, thought it was just a friend, but not from the way they were sitting. I heard that she did run around. Oh well, who cares, none of my business, & you would tell me to mind it wouldn't you Ducky.

Maybe I will have a letter tomorrow. Be getting the pictures at the end of the month. I'm looking forward to yours. Well, Sweetheart, I'm so tired, can hardly direct this pen, so good night you hunk of a man, & I love you so. xxxxxxx. See you tomorrow.

Tues. eve. 7 pm.

Hello Darling, here I am at last, haven't had much time to write more so maybe now I can finish, just put the boss to bed, (Mike) but he won't go to sleep right away, but I know where he is. You should hear him call Margo, he puts more emphasis on the 'go', sounds sometimes like a 'k', but it sounds cute anyway.

Guess Mammie went back to work yesterday, she had been home all the week before. She needed the rest, did her good.

Tomorrow night I am going to the dance at the I.C. with Phyl Fricker, Jo Down, & Ada Graham, do you remember her. She used to be Ada Ellis. Her husband was killed overseas last August. They didn't have a dance last time on account they had the mumps. Nora told me last night. Fred is in Holland now.

170

Well, Sweetheart, I'm broke again, but that isn't anything new is it dear, but guess can wait until the end of the week.

What a day, rain, rain, rain, all day & still raining.

Guess had better get the other half of the Dymond family washed & put to bed much to her regret, as she doesn't like going to bed any more, guess cause it is so light now. I'm still trying to get a gas stove heater.

Well, Sweetheart, guess will close now, & do some work, maybe will have a letter from you tomorrow, here's hoping, - a song on the radio now, - "Counting the Days", who don't.

Remember, I love you very much, or are you tired of me saying so; (ha), just wait until I get a hold of you, - Keep Happy, my Darling.

Love as always, Phyllis, Margo & Michael
xxxx

Too Old For The Draft

Now I am old and feeble,
My pilot light is out,
What used to be my sex appeal
Is now my water spout.

I used to be embarrassed,
To make the thing behave,
For every single morning
Would sit up and watch me shave.

But now I'm growing older,
And it sure gives me the blues,
To see the thing hang down my leg
And watch me shine my shoes.

You may know this, but show it to some of the boys. ??

Give them my regards,
Love, Phyl

Captain Donald W Dymond, 1945

Margo and Phyllis Dymond, 1942

Monday, Apr. 30/45

Dearest Don:

Guess it is about time I was writing again, don't you. Don't know what is the matter with me. I'm just crazy or "somepen!" This boy of yours is a problem, he is so full of pep & energy. He just goes from one thing to the other, & keeps you busy following him around.

I told you he likes to take the tubes out of the radio, & don't think I don't try and stop him, cause I do, & if you or somebody has any suggestions please forward to me.

Well, he kept getting these tubes out & hitting them together until one is no good. I took it in to have it tested for sure, & it isn't, so he hasn't right now, but

it would play without it, so Sunday morning while I was at church he takes the other one, & ruins it, so now the radio won't play. Some kid. Here's the latest. Mom just made a cake, & it was sitting on the oven. So Mike takes it down, & has eaten all the top off. He can stand things hot, like you drinking hot tea. I tell you he is one persons work. He just pushed Margo's toys & things she had on the chair, all on the floor, so now he is sitting on the chair. The Boss. If I told you all the things he does, & gets into it would fill a book, and you can lick and talk to him, but he doesn't care, just smiles at you, so wicked. Mom says if you make any more boys, she will cut your whistle off. There just won't be any more _period._ I've had my fill of kids.

I went to the I.C. dance last week, & had a good time, & found myself a boyfriend. I dance with him most of the time. He reminded me of you quite a bit, & he wanted to take me home in a taxi, but I go with Phyl, & don't like to do it. So he wanted to take me to a show, so I told him maybe, & he asked for my phone number, & I told him 123, & he looked at me and laughed, he wouldn't laugh if he called it. So I gave him my right one, & he is going to call me tomorrow. Is that all right to you dear, so if you hear some gossip about your wife, that is what it will be. The war news looks good, & we hear so many rumors, but they don't fizz on me, not until the real one. The weather is still cold, have been burning coal all this month. Will be glad when it is warmer, so the kids can go out to play. I can't find that last letter I had from you, with that girls address in it. I took it up for P. &

M. to read, & can't remember whether she gave it back or not. She says yes, & I've looked here, but I may find it yet.

Tonight Mother is giving a party for Doreen, so she can invite all her girlfriends over, so they have a get together before she goes home, cause it may come any day & just give her two days to get ready, & that isn't very long to say good-bye to your friends.

Have you seen any of the boys lately? & how are you doing. I was going to collect some things for a box. There isn't very much change here in the big city, still looks the same. Now the sun is shining. First it shines, then it rains. Do you know what a constipated cat is? - A tight pussy.

Do you know why a man's balls are always cold, cause their two below.

The mail man just come, but just brought me my magazine.

Now, Tues. 2.15.

Mom has just taken Margo out to the show, & I just have Wayne and Mike. Shirley has Jimmie, & what a relief, as he is a pest, to me anyway. We had a pretty good time last night, or at least Doreen & her friends & they gave her some nice presents. Myself I have the sniffles, or cold in the head, & the kids have running noses, this silly weather, liable to have anything. No mail from so far, so have none to ans. Guess will go to the show tonight, if my boy-friend calls. (ha,ha).

Did my weekly washing this morning. If my furniture & things keep falling, or coming apart, will have to give them to the junk man & start all over again. Now it is my cedar chest, two places on it have to be fixed, & last night Margo sitting on the bed took my good comb that goes with the set *you gave me, & broke about six teeth out of it, now it looks like an old hag.*

Well my Darling, guess this all for now hoping you are well, & doing o.k. considering the situation, so with all my love,

As ever yours,

Love you dearly,
Phyllis, Margo & Michael
xxxxxx

These last two letters were returned to Phyllis on May 8 and 12/45 respectively. Don was killed in action on the day the second one was written.

Margo, age 5 and Michael age 3, 1947

AFTERWARD

There were many difficult letters that dad wrote, a few that were daunting even to begin. I am sure that each got more arduous, certainly when you are overwhelmed with love and nowhere to put it. Beyond the "I will love you forever," and days running each seamlessly into the next and weeks at a time, a monotonous regularity must set in as reality collides with hope, and hope is all there is. This is an authenticity far too real. A reality you would never wish to experience. It's all so disparate.

How does sullen become strong? How did those who had been in England for longer than dad survive it and the training? And they were nowhere near the fight. There had been much discussion it would appear about the war being over soon...Jerry is on the run...Churchill is in Canada right now putting together a plan to end it all...the Russians and Americans are pushing Jerry hard. And it goes on yet there is no end in sight.

There is much sadness between the lines in all of Dad's letters. He feels it is his job to keep mom's spirits up. He feels strongly about this as it was he that volunteered for duty, of which he clearly speaks. At times they were a cover for his sadness and maybe even a little regret for having made such a sacrifice. But that is what war is...a sacrifice.

I felt that I would not be able to do his life justice, the very short one he had, most of which was, sadly, in the service of war. But he was not alone. Many did as he and volunteered knowing full well that their effort may be what keeps all the disease that Hitler was from showing up on Canadian shores. He also had a family that came into being and grew while he was away. And even though he did see and hold his daughter, never was he to gaze into the eyes of his son. He worked very diligently to keep their spirits up. Being where he was he felt strongly, again, was of his doing, not his families…and so that role was his to play. Hope you, the reader, enjoyed the read.

LIFE LETTERS

All the stuff that comprises our daily lives was not missed by Donald and Phyllis. Not really. Shock and surprise, wonder, laughter, intimacy and tenderness were there. Tears of joy, birth and fear, they were there too. And faith, hope and love endured the test of time and distance.

They were together for four months after their marriage. There were thirty months when just brief visits - leaves while training and guarding in Canada - to tend to family business and conceive two children were savored. And eleven months in both England and the war's front in Europe which ended in tragedy.

Letters became their life together. Hundreds of letters were written that they both laughed and cried over, fifty-four of which appear verbatim in the forgoing story.

The desolation and melancholy of a world war creeps into all lives. No one is left untouched as our humanity is outstripped. For Phyllis, the never knowing in the darkest moments weighed heavily on her soul. And there were two young children.

Reading the papers, waiting for a call while huddled by the radio at all hours, wrapped in fear and hope became her daily bread. These were extraordinary times.

Their life was letters...life letters.

ABOUT THE AUTHOR

Michael W Dymond, the son of Donald and Phyllis, was born and raised in Chatham, Ontario, Canada. He had been given hundreds of love letters by his mother that she had received from Donald while he was away serving his country and humanity during WWII. From this amazing collection of letters he wrote this short book with love and in the memory of a father he never knew.